The Ultimate Chocolate Cookie Book

OTHER BOOKS BY BRUCE WEINSTEIN AND MARK SCARBROUGH

The Ultimate Muffin Book
The Ultimate Potato Book
The Ultimate Brownie Book
The Ultimate Shrimp Book
Cooking for Two: 125 Recipes for Every Day and Those Special Nights

OTHER BOOKS BY BRUCE WEINSTEIN

The Ultimate Candy Book
The Ultimate Ice Cream Book
The Ultimate Party Drink Book

From Chocolate
 Melties to Whoopie Pies,
Chocolate Biscotti to Black
 and Whites, with Dozens
of Chocolate Chip Cookies
 and Hundreds More

The
Ultimate
Chocolate
Cookie
Book

BRUCE WEINSTEIN AND
MARK SCARBROUGH

WILLIAM MORROW
An Imprint of HarperCollinsPublishers

To the members of the Stonewall Chorale in New York City.
Hundreds of test batches later, you're still first in the nation.

HarperCollins books may be purchased for educational, business, or sales promotional use. For information please write: Special Markets Department, HarperCollins Publishers Inc., 10 East 53rd Street, New York, NY 10022.

FIRST EDITION

Design by Renato Stanisic

Printed on acid-free paper

Library of Congress Cataloging-in-Publication Data

Weinstein, Bruce, 1960–
    The ultimate chocolate cookie book : from chocolate melties to whoopie pies, chocolate biscotti to black and whites, with dozens of chocolate chip cookies and hundreds more / Bruce Weinstein and Mark Scarbrough.—1st ed.
        p.   cm.
    ISBN 0-06-056274-9
    1. Cookies.   2. Cookery (Chocolate)   I. Scarbrough, Mark.   II. Title.
TX772.W43   2004
641.8'654—dc22

                                            2004042424

04 05 06 07 08 WBC/QW 10 9 8 7 6 5 4 3 2 1

CONTENTS

ACKNOWLEDGMENTS

To make a chocolate cookie book, start with a patient, savvy, generous editor such as Harriet Bell, the one ingredient without which nothing else will cohere. Make sure the manuscript falls into the hands of her assistant, Lucy Baker, who edits and fields endless questions; let it rise under the direction of Sonia Greenbaum whose copyediting is measured and firm. Use chocolate provided generously and unstintingly by Robert Steinberg of ScharffenBerger Chocolate Makers. As you're mixing it up, have a great agent like Susan Ginsburg at Writers House and the hyper-competent Rachel Spector to oversee the process start to finish. That ever-important sheen on the piece can only be made by Roberto de Vicq de Cumptich, William Staehle, Elizabeth Ackerman, and Renato Stanisic. And once the manuscript begins to gather into a ball, make sure there's the production team of Ann Cahn, Karen Lumley, Leah Carlson-Stanisic, and Jessica Peskay to see that it comes out just right. And once out of the oven, always have Alisande Morales, Carrie Bachman, Jonathan Schwartz, and Bobbilyn Jones at the ready to make sure everyone gets a taste. Have Beth Shepard on hand, too, to make sure your cookies pack well over the long distances of various media waves.

INTRODUCTION

A MATCH MADE IN HOLLAND

Doing cooking demos and teaching classes around the country, we've learned one thing: no one ever tires of chocolate.

No wonder then that sometime during a demo at the International Chocolate Show in New York City, the idea hit us for an ultimate chocolate cookie book. We were making a particularly decadent treat: brownie turtle sundaes—brown sugar brownies, truffle ice cream, caramel sauce, and pecan bark. Somewhere between the brownies and the bark, we must have had the world's first joint beatific moment—we already knew we wanted to write a cookie book, but why waste time on anything that wasn't chocolate?

For a while after that, we lived in a kind of chocolate Paradise: bittersweet, semisweet, chips, melted, grated, chopped. We had chocolate chip cookies galore, macaroons and chocolate sandwich cookies, biscotti and chocolate tea biscuits, whole trays of them, cooling on the counters and the dining room table, then rather unceremoniously dumped into plastic bags and brought to friends all across New York City. Not once did anyone turn us down.

Chocolate and cookies. It's a match so natural, so obvious, it's hard to believe how modern it is. 1828, in fact. We can thank a Dutch chemist, Coenraad Johannes

Van Houten, for almost every recipe in this book—not the recipes themselves, mind you, but the mere fact that they exist.

Before Van Houten, chocolate was almost exclusively a drink, hot or cold, express from the New World—not hot chocolate as we now know it, with warm milk; but a drink made with water, thick and bitter, like coffee, made by stirring the ground chocolate into hot water, and then drinking it without straining it. The Maya and Aztecs combined the fermented, ground chocolate beans with maize, spices, and water, then poured the concoction from a great height into smaller pots, thereby creating a muddy beverage with a viscous foam.

The conquistadors and other colonialists simply followed suit. After much ecclesiastical debate, Europeans developed a taste for this thick sludge (no maize for them, but other thickeners, like farina) and its heady foam (no pouring either— they beat the mixture with a small wooden whisk). However, they made one telling innovation. By the 1500s, sugar was a Western craze. So they sweetened the drink, now perfumed with everything from vanilla to musk(!), and drank to their hearts' content. Chocolate was soon the beverage of choice in the Spanish court. Versailles was known to have a never-ending string of pots and chocolate service at all hours. And chocolate houses (the forerunners of coffeehouses) sprang up thick and fast in London's central business district.

The royals and businessmen were quaffing a greasy, grainy mess. First, the chocolate they used didn't dissolve; even powdered, it fell out of suspension and ended up at the bottom of the cup (again, like grounds in coffee). Second, chocolate naturally contains cocoa butter. This fat also didn't hold in suspension; it rose to the top of the drink, making an oily slick in the foam. To make matters worse, the cocoa butter itself had often gone rancid from improper storage and unscrupulous additives. It wasn't exactly savory fare. No wonder a stern, no-funny-business chemist from Holland was so interested in perfecting this prize from the New World.

Van Houten solved all these problems: fat, taste, and texture. He perfected a machine that could extract most of the cocoa butter from chocolate, thereby making a dry cake that could be pulverized without the attendant grease—thus, what we now call "cocoa powder." And he added an alkali to chocolate, thereby making it considerably darker in color but far less bitter in taste, as well as better able to mix in water—thus, what we now call "Dutch-processed cocoa powder."

For our purposes, it's a strange and wonderful coincidence that a Dutchman came up with the first truly usable and palatable chocolate. The Dutch, of course, are purported also to be the inventors of cookies. The very word "cookie" most likely comes from a Dutch word, *kookje,* or "small cake"—or (more accurately) "test cake," for a *kookje* was that bit of batter thrown onto the floor of an oven to test the heat. If the batter just sat there, the oven needed more time to heat up; if the *kookje* burned at the edges, the oven needed time to cool down. So we have the chocolate and we have the cookies in one country—but we don't yet have a chocolate cookie. That divine combination still had to wait.

Van Houten's cocoa-making process had an unwitting by-product: cocoa butter and lots of it. Manufacturers now had an excess which they could sell (many still do) to the cosmetic and pharmaceutical industries. But surely there was something one could do on a culinary front with that luscious left-over.

Pump it back into chocolate, of course. And that idea arose in a country that practically invented the sweet tooth: Great Britain. Less than twenty years after Van Houten applied for his patent, an enterprising Quaker businessman, Joseph Storrs Fry, already the owner of a small chocolate concern, discovered that he could mix sugar and cocoa solids with melted cocoa butter and create a thick, luscious mixture that could be molded and hardened—in other words, the world's first chocolate bar.

But baking with chocolate still proved an elusive notion. Sure, people had cooked with chocolate before. The Marquis de Sade, trapped in the Bastille, sent endless letters to his wife, imploring her to have their personal chef send chocolate cakes while he waited for his trial. But these concoctions were rarities, not the norm. Chocolate was a drink—period. An aristocratic, elitist drink. Any use of it in ordinary baking would cross well-established boundaries. (Heaven forfend, that's what de Sade did!) It would take the thinking of someone who didn't follow the rules. The kind of thinking Americans excel at.

The first breakthrough happened in 1912. The National Biscuit Company (aka Nabisco), looking for a follow-up hit to Barnum's Animal Crackers, introduced two chocolate disks sandwiching a cream filling: the Oreo, the first chocolate cookie craze. Lines were said to form at markets well before dawn as people waited for the next shipment of what has since become the best-selling chocolate cookie ever, with more than 7.5 billion sold each year.

But the real conflagration for home bakers came in 1930 when Ruth Wakefield made culinary history with the first chocolate chip cookie. One afternoon at the Toll House Inn in Whitman, Massachusetts, Wakefield cut up a chocolate bar, dropped it in her butter cookies, and invented an icon. But this was no happy accident. Wakefield was an entrepreneur who ran one of the most successful tourist businesses on the East Coast; she was also a trained nutritionist. Nestlé had sent her bars of chocolate because the company was looking for a new sensation, something that would market their product to new heights. Ruth willingly obliged. And the rest? As they say, it's history.

It's a short hop from Oreo and Tollhouse cookies to a book like this, dedicated to the chocolate cookie in all its forms, whether made with cocoa powder or melted chocolate. We hope these are recipes you can come back to time and again—loads of chocolate chip cookies (believe it or not, the Vegan Chocolate Chip Cookies are our favorite), lots of sandwich cookies, some down-home treats like Chocolate Marshmallow Cookies (our version of Mallomars), and even a few foofy treats like Chocolate Tuiles. Soon, you'll be doing your own demos—in front of your kids, friends, or family. And you'll learn the same thing we did: no one ever tires of chocolate, especially when it's in cookies.

A Word About This Book

The Ultimate Chocolate Cookie Book is another installment in the *Ultimate* series, one that began with *The Ultimate Ice Cream Book* and has continued through various incarnations, including party drinks, candy, shrimp, brownies, potatoes, and muffins. Chocolate cookies are a natural next step in this parade of America's favorite fun foods, all fast yet homey.

Like the other ultimate books, this one presents a series of base recipes arranged alphabetically: Almond Coconut Cookies, Banana Chocolate Chip Cookies, etc. Most of the base recipes are followed by variations, usually an added or substituted ingredient or two: a little mint extract, some white chocolate chips, things like that. A few cookies are such classics, or the dough is so delicate, that variations proved impossible. These we've let stand on their own. But in the end, our notion for the *Ultimate* books holds true even here: we give you recipes you can customize to your personal taste—or style.

That said, we do have predilections, best confessed up front. Some of our chocolate cookies are not as sweet as some others you may have bought or made. If you have an achingly active sweet tooth, search out our recipes for Butterscotch Chocolate Chip Cookies (page 39), Triple Chocolate Chocolate Chip Cookies (page 217), and the like. However, we believe cutting down on the sugar a bit lets the dense, rich taste of the chocolate shine through, particularly if you're already using semisweet chocolate in the recipe. It's not that we're sugarphobic (ice cream, candy, and brownie books should put to rest any fears). We're just addicted to chocolate.

What's more, we like crunchy chocolate chip cookies and softer dark chocolate cookies. If you're not exactly in synch with our tastes, we have some ways around them, as you'll see in the variations—ideas, that is, for turning crunchy cookies into cakey ones and vice versa.

Still, you glance through the base recipes, looking for something to scratch that cookie itch, and you want just the right thing. To help you decide, we've created a "crunch-o-meter" at the head of each recipe.

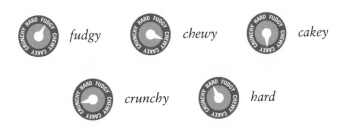

Some cookies fall between these markings, as you'll see—halfway between cakey and crunchy, say. And any batch of cookies can be affected by the day's humidity (drier days produce crisper cookies). The baking time of any batch can also be modified for somewhat different results (shorter is usually softer; longer, crunchier). But this crunch-o-meter should give you a general idea of which cookies are which.

All hints and notations aside, the joy of baking is the joy of the unexpected. It's an organic process, like life: you get what you make and what's been made of it. And that's enough of a reason to bake up a batch of cookies. Besides eating them, of course.

On Baking Chocolate Cookies

Tips for Success

Getting Started

1. Position the oven racks as directed.
A few recipes ask you to position the oven rack in the center of the oven; a few others, in the top third only; and a very few, in odd configurations like the center and top third. Most, however, ask you to stack the racks: one in the top third, the other in the bottom third. In this case, don't place one rack directly over the other. Space them out for better air flow.

2. Preheat the oven.
Cookies require even heat to bake properly. Let the oven preheat for 15 minutes, so it's good and hot before you put the cookies in.

3. Prepare the baking sheets as directed.
As schoolmarmish as it sounds, there's really only one thing we can say: follow the recipe. If it asks you to grease the sheet, don't skip this step, even if you're using nonstick baking sheets. A thin layer of fat between the metal and the cookies will yield crisper, crunchier bottoms, more in keeping with that standard cookie texture.

Don't grease a baking sheet if the recipe calls for parchment paper or a silicone baking mat. The cookies will most likely burn—or spread too much and turn into giant, flat disks because the circumference won't harden before the batter begins to soften.

And don't substitute parchment paper or a silicone baking mat for a greased cookie sheet. Both linings place a layer of insulation between the batter and the baking sheet, insulation that is necessary for delicate tuiles and fortune cookies, thin cookies that need to bake quickly but also need protection from direct heat.

Working with Chocolate

1. Chop the chocolate.

Chocolate is sold in either 1-ounce squares (for convenience) or larger blocks (for economics). In neither case is it sold for immediate melting. Even the 1-ounce squares are too large to melt evenly: the edges will scorch before the middle softens.

To get the chocolate into a form that will melt successfully, line your work surface with wax or parchment paper (to catch the small shards) and chop the chocolate using a large chef's knife or a chocolate chopper (see page 15). Press down into the chocolate, cutting it into pieces about the size of half an almond.

You can also chop chocolate in a food processor, but the results vary, particularly if the bowl is not scrupulously dry or if the machine heats the chocolate in any way, causing it to melt. Fit the machine with the coarse grating disk, then feed large chunks of the chocolate into the feed tube and press down with the plunger as the blade whirs.

2. In most cases, melt the chocolate early in the recipe.

Melted chocolate needs to cool slightly, usually for 5 minutes, maybe for 10, so that (1) it doesn't liquefy the butterfat in the batter, (2) it doesn't scramble the eggs, and (3) it doesn't seize when it comes in contact with the liquid ingredients. When chocolate seizes, it breaks into stiff, stubby threads and a dark, thin liquid. Quite frankly, this is the worst thing that can happen to chocolate.

When melting chocolate, stir it frequently. Semisweet and bittersweet chocolate both hold their shape even while melting internally. If you wait to stir until they appear to have turned to liquid, you have waited too long—the chocolate is scorched (and bitter) on the bottom.

There are some exceptions to this melt-it-early rule—the Almond Coconut Cookies, for example. These exceptions involve special uses for the chocolate, like making a chocolate coating or a ganache filling for sandwich cookies.

3. If the chocolate seizes, hope for the best.

Melting chocolate seizes if even a tiny amount of water gets into the mix. The water usually comes from steam rising from the bottom part of the double boiler and condensing into the mixture, or from a few droplets in an incompletely dried bowl or pot that holds the melting chocolate, or from an improperly dried spatula or wooden spoon.

If the chocolate seizes in the double boiler as it's being melted, you may be able to repair it by beating 1 or 2 teaspoons of warmed, heavy cream into the mess—but you have to hope for the best.

If the melted chocolate seizes as it's poured into the batter, beat the mixture quickly and steadily. Often, the presence of the egg's proteins and naturally occurring lecithin will help the chocolate readhere in the batter. The cookies may be grainier and tougher—but the difference here will be far less than if the chocolate seizes in the double boiler while it's being melted.

4. Take extra care when working with bittersweet chocolate.

Bittersweet chocolate has a significantly lower amount of sugar—this reduction can lead the chocolate to seize more readily than semisweet brands. (See page 17 for a discussion of the various types of chocolate.) Cookies made with bittersweet chocolate can also be drier and tougher than those made with semisweet chocolate. If your chocolate is a high-percentage bittersweet chocolate (between 72 percent and 85 percent cocoa liqueur), we recommend increasing the granulated sugar in the recipe by 1 teaspoon per ounce of chocolate used.

Making Cookies

1. Mix the dry ingredients in a separate bowl.
Admittedly, this seems like a fussy step, but doing so will allow the baking soda, baking powder, salt, and/or cocoa powder to be distributed evenly throughout the batter. A whisk is the best tool for the job.

2. Sift the cocoa powder.
Always sift cocoa powder through a fine-mesh strainer to get rid of any lumps formed by excessive humidity or other moisture. Press any lumps with the back of a wooden spoon to break them into powder.

We rarely ask you to sift the flour. A couple of recipes call for this step, but they have special pleadings due to the consistency of the batter, usually cakier than that of the standard cookie.

3. Have the eggs at room temperature.
Cold eggs can cause melted chocolate to seize. They can also lead to tough cookies since they can cause the softened butter to firm up unexpectedly, just when it should be adhering to the proteins. To bring eggs to room temperature, set them out on the counter for 15 minutes (while the oven is preheating, perhaps) or submerge them in a bowl of warm (not hot) water for 5 minutes.

4. Use cool butter unless the recipe indicates otherwise.
Some cooking myths refuse to die. One of the most persistent is the one about making batters with room-temperature butter, which could be anywhere between 70°F and 85°F, depending on your personal taste and monthly heating budget.

When making a batter, you beat the butter to aerate it, to get tiny air bubbles into the batter's structure. Problem is, butterfat begins to melt around 68°F and can then no longer form a structure for the batter. If you want to trap air bubbles, you need the butter to be colder than 68°F.

We recommend taking the unsalted butter out of the refrigerator, cutting it into small pieces, and letting it stand for just 2 or 3 minutes. It will be cool, not cold.

Now beat it with an electric mixer at medium speed until softened, not runny. With a stand mixer, softening cool butter is no problem. If you have a handheld mixer, you can use the beaters like a pastry cutter to cut the butter into finer and finer pieces while beating.

5. Pack the brown sugar.

Brown sugar is coarser than granulated sugar, so it needs to be packed into measuring cups and spoons to avoid needless air pockets. Don't smash it down until the sugar's a rock; press down once with the back of a spoon, then fill the measuring cup or spoon again before leveling it off.

6. Avoid sticky utensils.

Sidestep a sink full of sticky utensils by weighing out the solid vegetable shortening. Put your mixing bowl on the kitchen scale, calibrate it to zero, then add enough shortening to come up to the recipe's required amount. Here's an easy reference chart:

> *1 tablespoon = 1/2 ounce*
> *2 tablespoons = 1 ounce*
> *1/4 cup (or 4 tablespoons) = 2 ounces*
> *1/2 cup (or 8 tablespoons) = 4 ounces*
> *1 cup (or 16 tablespoons) = 8 ounces*

To get sticky honey or molasses out of a measuring cup, first spray the cup lightly with nonstick spray, then measure out what you need. The fine coating will help the sticky liquid pour easily into the batter.

7. Let the electric mixer do most of the work—from softening the butter to mixing in the flour.

Some chefs still beat the butter by hand, then fold in the dry ingredients with a rubber spatula. But a mixer will get more air into the butter before it's above 68°F and loses its elasticity.

A mixer will also get the flour quickly into the batter before the glutens become sticky. It can also get a fine dusting of flour all over you and your kitchen. To avoid this cleanup nightmare, turn the beaters off before you add the flour, then beat at the lowest speed possible. If you're working in a bowl smaller than the large ones associated with stand mixers, add the flour in stages, a little at a time, so that it doesn't rise up above the bowl's rim as it's beaten in.

8. Reverse the baking sheets halfway during baking.
For the best air flow, we almost always ask you to rotate the baking sheets. If the recipe asks you to bake one sheet at a time, rotate it front to back, 180 degrees, halfway through baking. If you're using two, rotate each back to front, then reverse them, the one on the top rack to the bottom and vice versa.

What if you have only one baking sheet but the recipe calls for two? Stack the racks as directed. Begin baking with the sheet on the bottom rack; halfway through baking, rotate it front to back and move it to the upper rack.

All that said, if you have a convection oven with proven and efficient air flow, reversing the sheets is largely unnecessary.

9. Cool the baking sheets before making additional batches.
We have not written these recipes with any one-size baking sheet in mind. But because your sheets may be smaller than ours, you may need to bake additional batches of cookies to use up all the dough. Before you do, always let the baking sheets cool for at least 5 minutes before placing unbaked cookie dough on them. Hot baking sheets make batters spread, resulting in flattened, overbaked cookies. If the sheets need to be greased (and floured), do so again once they're cool. If you're using parchment paper, check to make sure it's not frizzled or dried out. If so, replace it with a new sheet of paper.

10. Store baked cookies as recommended.
At the end of each recipe, we've given our storage recommendations: at room temperature and in the freezer.

Make sure cookies have cooled completely before storing them. A safe bet is to leave them on the cooling racks for 2 hours. Then store the cookies in an airtight container at room temperature to preserve flavor and moisture. Seal a plastic container tightly, releasing any excess air. If you're using a cookie jar, make sure the lid's on tight. Store any iced cookies or fudgy cookies between sheets of wax paper.

Don't store soft and crisp cookies together at room temperature. The moisture in the soft ones will cause the crunchy ones to go limp.

Most cookies freeze extremely well. (The exceptions are those with gooey centers or some filled sandwich cookies.) To freeze cookies, store them in stacked layers between sheets of wax paper in freezer-safe, zip-closed bags or in plastic containers. To defrost, remove the frozen cookies from the bag and place them on a wire rack so that any melting ice crystals don't turn the bottoms soggy. Let the cookies sit in the open air for 15 to 20 minutes, but no more than 30 minutes, then store them at room temperature as indicated.

One warning: if you have a frost-free freezer, the cookies cannot stay in the freezer as long as we recommend, since the temperature comes up to 32°F (usually once a day) so the freezer will defrost. This fluctuation will lead to soggy cookies; store them no more than a couple weeks in a frost-free freezer.

Equipment

Most equipment you need to bake chocolate cookies is commonsensical: a wire whisk, rubber spatula, metal spatula, wooden spoon, and various bowls. Some things, however, may require a brief introduction.

BAKING SHEETS Technically, a cookie sheet is a large, flat baking sheet with one or two upturned edges, or maybe none at all; a baking sheet has four upturned edges. The latter is easier to handle (you can grab any side, provided you have a hot pad in hand), and its lipped edges will prevent round dough balls from slipping onto the kitchen floor or baked cookies from sliding into the oven.

Insulated baking sheets will indeed prevent cookies from burning. However, they can change the baking times dramatically, especially with short (i.e., dry) batters. If you have an insulated baking sheet, watch the times carefully—you may also try baking your cookies only in the bottom third of the oven to keep them from spreading too much as they bake.

CHOCOLATE CHOPPER This heavy-duty, rakelike tool is sold at some baking supply outlets and many kitchenware stores. Its tines are particularly adept at shearing blocks of chocolate into smaller chunks.

CHOCOLATE GRATER Some recipes ask you to grate the chocolate into the dough. A strange technique, admittedly, but this way the chocolate doesn't bog the dough with excess fat as it bakes, so the cookies don't spread out on the baking sheets. Use large chunks or whole squares of chocolate; grate them with the small holes of a box grater or a microplane, a device designed to grate cheese into fine filaments. In either case, mind your knuckles. Or use a clean Mouli grater, a Parmesan-cheese grater with a round inner tube. It grates the chocolate as you turn the handle—but make sure you use the cutting tube designed for fine grating, not the one for coarse bits. Some specialty cookware stores sell chocolate graters, which can make thin curls of chocolate—perfect provided you draw the grater across the chocolate in short strokes, thereby producing shards of chocolate, not big fancy curls.

DOUBLE BOILER This handy kitchen tool consists of one pot straddling a slightly deeper one. Why would you need such a device? Chocolate is temperamental—it scorches in no time—so a double boiler allows you to melt chocolate over indirect heat.

While the recipes that call for melted chocolate call for a double boiler, we also always offer an alternative. If there is only a small amount of chocolate to be melted, we give instructions for melting it in a microwave. For larger amounts, we offer a home fix-it contraption of a mixing bowl set over a similarly sized pot of simmering water. The one problem? The escaping steam in this less-than-perfectly-fitting system can give your fingers a nasty burn and can cause the chocolate to seize (see page 10). Watch the pot carefully, adjusting the heat under it to maintain a slow but steady boil.

ELECTRIC MIXER   A stand mixer is powerful enough to soften the butter before it begins to lose its elasticity. If you have a handheld mixer, place your mixing bowl in the sink, securing it in the drain so that it doesn't jump around while you're beating in the ingredients. You may have to beat some of the batters a minute or two longer than stated in the recipes to get to the right visual cue for the steps in the process.

KITCHEN SCALES   Of course, you can always rely on the 1-ounce squares of chocolate and the like—but if you buy in bulk, you'll have to have kitchen scales for accuracy's sake. Scales will also help you measure out shortening without the attendant sticky utensils (see page 12).

PASTRY BAG AND TIPS   A few of the fancier recipes ask you to pipe out the batter using a pastry bag and a specified round tip, in all cases either a ⅜-inch round tip or a ¾-inch round tip. Pastry bags and tips can be found at any baking supply or kitchenware store. We prefer disposable plastic pastry bags, rather than traditional cloth bags simply because disposable bags make cleanup a snap. You can also improvise with a zip-closed plastic bag by snipping a bottom corner to the required diameter, filling the bag with dough, and piping out as directed by squeezing the dough through the small hole you've made. This homemade pastry bag will yield perfectly acceptable if not absolutely perfect results.

ROLLING PIN   Buy one heavy enough that you don't have to press down and roll the dough out by brute force. In other words, let the pin do the work for you.

WIRE RACK FOR COOLING   A sturdy wire rack is essential for cooling cookies once they're baked. The mesh allows air to circulate under the cookies so they don't turn soggy.

Some Special Ingredients

Cookies don't require many fussy ingredients. Most are well within a baker's pantry. That said, some may have a few tricks or secrets—as you'll see in this short list.

Almond paste

Sometimes sold as "marzipan," this concoction of ground almonds and sugar (with glucose often added for a smooth texture) is found in the baking aisle of most supermarkets. Look for fresh, soft tubes—a squeeze will tell you if the paste has hardened to a useless lump. If yours in the pantry has, remove the paste from the tube and soften it in the microwave in 10-second increments—but hope for the best because the almond oil can easily fall out of suspension, creating a mess.

Baking powder and baking soda

The acid and the base in baking powder slowly duke it out over time, despite the presence of cornstarch, which is supposed to break up the fight. To test if yours is still good, mix 1 teaspoon in 1 cup of hot water. If it bubbles vigorously, it's good to go.

Humidity can greatly compromise baking soda. To test if yours is active, mix ¼ teaspoon in 2 tablespoons vinegar. If it bubbles vigorously, you're ready to bake.

As a rule of thumb, replace baking powder every 4 months; baking soda, every 6 months. Never use the baking soda you've kept in the refrigerator to absorb odors—the resulting cookies will taste like onions, fish, or goodness knows what.

Chocolate

There's really only one rule when you buy chocolate: buy the best you can comfortably afford. Good-quality chocolate makes all the difference.

If you're going to be making a lot of cookies—say, a holiday production line—consider buying chocolate in bulk from a baking supply store. A 5-pound block is more economical than an endless parade of 1-ounce squares—more economical, that is, if you're actually going to use it.

Time compromises chocolate. For one thing, chocolate "blooms." It gets a superficial white film caused by the cocoa butter coming out of suspension—it's still acceptable for melting, but not good for turning into chunks for cookies because its texture has been compromised. Chocolate also picks up pantry odors and flavors. What's more, it can turn grainy because of humidity and excess moisture dissolving the sugar in suspension.

Better-quality chocolate is often sold with a percentage indicator, which marks the amount of cocoa liqueur (cocoa solids and cocoa butter) as measured against other ingredients (mostly sugar, vanilla, and some kind of chemical enhancer like lecithin).

Unsweetened chocolate is sometimes sold as "99 percent." It's also sometimes sold as "baking chocolate." This should not be confused with the brand "Baker's Chocolate," although Baker's Chocolate does make baking chocolate!

While standards vary, for the purposes of this book, semisweet chocolate is anything in the 50 percent to 69 percent range; bittersweet, anything in the 70 percent to 90 percent range. As a general rule, the lower the percent, the sweeter the cookies; the higher the percent, the less sweet.

White chocolate is just cocoa butter, no brown cocoa solids. The cocoa butter is blended with sugar, milk solids, vanilla, and stabilizers. If possible, buy pure white chocolate, not cut with hydrogenated shortening.

Most chocolate chips are made of semisweet chocolate; some gourmet stores and the like sell chips or chunks of bittersweet chocolate. In almost all cases, either of these chips will work in a recipe that calls for chocolate chips added directly to a batter.

Chocolate chunks are only called for by name in one recipe (Chocolate Chunk Cookies, page 61), but you could use chocolate chunks in any of the recipes that call for chocolate chips (for a complete list, see page 22). Chunks will yield a cookie with larger chocolate pockets, but not necessarily chocolate in every bite.

You can make your own chips or chunks by chopping chocolate squares or blocks with a chocolate chopper or a heavy chef's knife. Cut the chocolate into chunks about the size of semisweet chocolate morsels by pressing steadily but gently into the chocolate, using the tines of the chopper or the point of the knife.

Some home cooks melt chocolate chips when a recipe calls for melted chocolate. While this is perfectly acceptable, the results will again depend on the quality of chocolate a baker uses.

In terms of weight and volume measurements in the book, chocolate chips are always called for by volume (that is, in cup amounts—1½ cups, 3 cups, etc.) because (1) many of us buy chips in bulk from various warehouse retailers, and (2) volume is a reliable and convenient indicator for various additives (chips, raisins, nuts, and so forth) once a batter is formed. While the size and density of chocolate chips vary widely, a 12-ounce package of semisweet chips is about 2 cups.

That said, we call for all other chocolate by weight, not volume—that is, 1 ounce, 4 ounces, etc. We do this because (1) all chocolate other than chips is sold by weight, whether in 1-ounce squares or larger blocks, and (2) chocolate used to create a batter's structure must be measured by weight for accuracy's sake.

Cocoa powder

Cocoa powder is pulverized, dried cocoa solids. Contrary to popular belief, it is not fat-free. Rather, some fat has been retained in the process.

Cocoa powder is available in two forms: (1) "Dutch-processed," in which an alkali has been added to the cocoa nibs during production, producing a darker, less acidic cocoa powder; and (2) "natural cocoa powder," not doped and thus a powder that is lighter in appearance but with a taste ironically more like fine dark chocolate. A good larder, of course, will stock both kinds. If we have a preference, it's stated in the ingredients list.

Coconut

Sweetened shredded coconut is a familiar baking product to many of us, found in the baking aisle of almost every supermarket. Look for moist, soft flakes in a sealed plastic bag.

Unsweetened coconut chips are available at many gourmet markets as well as at most health food stores and is sometimes labeled "desiccated unsweetened coconut." These chips, some wide and others in shards depending on the packaging, are best when dry, not soft and pliable from improper storage and excess humidity.

Dried spices

All have a shelf life, usually between 2 and 4 months, depending on how volatile the spices' natural oils are. Store spices in a cool, dark place away from the stove. Always smell them before using—and replace with new bottles regularly.

Solid vegetable shortening

Choose a product made only from vegetable oils. We do not recommend lard in these recipes. (See page 12 for a tip on measuring the shortening.)

Sugar

Unless otherwise indicated, all sugar called for is granulated sugar.

Brown sugar is a mixture of molasses and granulated sugar (dark brown sugar has a little more molasses by weight; light brown, a little less). Unfortunately, this added moisture can cause brown sugar to clump and harden. There are two ways to soften it. For a long-term solution, place an apple wedge in the bag, seal it tightly, and store for about 2 days, or until softened. For a quick solution, place a partially sealed plastic bag filled with brown sugar in the microwave and heat on high in 10-second increments until the mixture softens. (The quicker method will produce less even results, with some knots of sugar still intact.)

Confectioners' sugar (called "powdered sugar" by some, or "icing sugar" in Great Britain and often in Canada) is granulated sugar that has been pulverized to a powder. It is combined with cornstarch (up to 3 percent by weight) to prevent its sticking together. The "X" marker on the package represents how small the grains are: the higher the number, the finer the grains. Any sold in large supermarkets are acceptable for the recipes in this book (usually from 4X to 10X).

Sanding sugar is a coarse sugar, sometimes colored, designed to give cookies a decorative coating, since it's coarse enough to resist melting. Choose the colors you prefer; baking-supply stores have a larger selection than supermarkets.

Coarse sugar has very large crystals, like coarse sea-salt crystals. It's also a decorative tool—it will not melt during the short baking time cookies undergo.

Superfine sugar is, of course, its dead opposite. Superfine sugar is used mostly for bar drinks—it dissolves in seconds without the added cornstarch in confectioners' sugar, which would cloud the drinks. Superfine sugar can also be used in flat, thin, crunchy cookies that must have absolutely no graininess when baked. If not found in the baking aisle, it can sometimes be found with the bar and drink mixes.

Vanilla extract
Although cheaper, imitation vanilla pales in comparison to the real thing. We suggest a splurge—because good chocolate deserves good vanilla.

High-Altitude Baking

Foods dry out more quickly at higher altitudes. On average, store cookies at room temperature for 1 day less than suggested. Flour is also drier, thanks to the lack of humidity, so more moisture is needed to make a successful batter. Follow this chart for any recipe changes:

Above	Reduce the baking powder or baking soda by	Reduce the sugar by	Add this much more liquid, or this much milk with the egg(s)
3,000 feet	⅛ teaspoon	½ tablespoon	1 tablespoon
5,000 feet	¼ teaspoon	1 tablespoon	2 tablespoons
7,500 feet	¼ teaspoon	2 tablespoons	3 tablespoons

Specialty Lists of Cookies

We've alphabetized the recipes so you don't have to turn to the index to find what you want. Sometimes, however, you may want a specific thing—and we've found that chocolate cookie lovers often want very specific things. So here's an easy reference list to some of the recipes, not by alphabetical title, but by type of cookie. Look up individual recipes alphabetically in the chapter that follows.

Biscotti
Chocolate Biscotti • Chocolate Chip Biscotti • Chocolate Hazelnut Biscotti • Espresso Chocolate Chip Biscotti • Low-Fat Chocolate Biscotti

Chocolate Chip Cookies (not any cookie made with chocolate chips, but those that have the classic chocolate-chip-cookie texture)
Banana Chocolate Chip Cookies • Butterscotch Chocolate Chip Cookies • Chocolate Chip Oatmeal Cookies • Chocolate Chocolate Chip Cookies • Chocolate Chunk Cookies • Classic Chocolate Chip Cookies • Coconut Chocolate Chip Cookies • Dairy-Free Chocolate Chip Cookies • Ginger Chocolate Chip Cookies • Gluten-Free Chocolate Chip Cookies • Honey Chocolate Chip Cookies • Maple Chocolate Chip Cookies • Peanut Butter Chocolate Chip Cookies • Peppermint Chocolate Chip Cookies • Potato Chip Chocolate Chip Cookies • Pumpkin Chocolate Chip Cookies • Soft Chocolate Chip Oatmeal Cookies • Sweet Potato Chocolate Chip Cookies • Tofu Chocolate Chip Cookies • Triple Chocolate Chocolate Chip Cookies • Vegan Chocolate Chip Cookies • White Chocolate Chocolate Chip Cookies

Chocolate Coconut Cookies (coconut is part of the base recipe, not added in a variation)
Almond Coconut Cookies • Chocolate Coconut and Pecan Cookies • Chocolate Coconut Cookies • Chocolate Coconut Macaroons • Coconut Chocolate Chip Cookies • Dairy-Free Chocolate Chip Cookies

Chocolate Oatmeal Cookies
Banana Chocolate Chip Cookies • Chocolate Chip Oatmeal Cookies • Chocolate Oatmeal Raisin Cookies • Dairy-Free Chocolate Chip Cookies • Honey Chocolate Chip Cookies • Soft Chocolate Chip Oatmeal Cookies • Vegan Chocolate Chip Cookies

Chocolate Cookies Made with Nuts (nuts are part of the base recipe, not a variation)
Almond Coconut Cookies • Chocolate Almond Horns • Chocolate Chews • Chocolate Chip Biscotti • Chocolate Coconut and Pecan Cookies • Chocolate Hazelnut Biscotti • Chocolate

Hazelnut Sandwich Cookies • Chocolate Jam Thumbprints • Chocolate Lace Sandwich Cookies • Chocolate Linzer Cookies • Chocolate Meringue Caps • Chocolate Meringues • Chocolate Pinwheels • Chocolate Sandies • Chocolate Truffle Sandwich Cookies • Chocolate Tuiles • Ganache Thumbprints • Low-Fat Chocolate Biscotti • Mexican Chocolate Walnut Cookies • Spumetti

Dairy-Free Chocolate Cookies
Chocolate Almond Horns • Chocolate Chews • Chocolate Chip Meringues • Chocolate Coconut Macaroons • Chocolate Cream Sandwich Cookies • Chocolate Fortune Cookies • Chocolate Gingerbread Men • Chocolate Gingersnaps • Chocolate Meringues • Chocolate Mint Sandwich Cookies • Chocolate Sandies • Chocolate Snickerdoodles • Chocolate Tea Cookies • Dairy-Free Chocolate Chip Cookies • French Macaroons • Nearly Nonfat Chocolate Cookies • Potato Chip Chocolate Chip Cookies • Spumetti • Tofu Chocolate Chip Cookies • Vegan Chocolate Chip Cookies

Gluten-Free Chocolate Cookies (if using gluten-free vanilla)
Chocolate Chip Meringues • Chocolate Coconut Macaroons • Chocolate Meringues • French Macaroons • Fudge Meringues • Gluten-Free Chocolate Chip Cookies • Spumetti

Sandwich Cookies
Chocolate Truffle Sandwich Cookies • Cats' Tongues • Chocolate Cream Sandwich Cookies • Chocolate Hazelnut Sandwich Cookies • Chocolate Lace Sandwich Cookies • Chocolate Linzer Cookies • Chocolate Mint Sandwich Cookies • Chocolate Peanut Butter Cream Sandwiches • Chocolate Ravioli Cookies • Chocolate Truffle Sandwich Cookies • French Macaroons • Whoopie Pies

Dropped Cookies
Banana Chocolate Chip Cookies • Big Soft Chocolate Cookies • Black Black and Whites • Brownie Drops • Butterscotch Chocolate Chip Cookies • Chocolate Chews • Chocolate Meringues • Chocolate Chocolate Chip Cookies • Chocolate Chunk Cookies • Chocolate Oatmeal Raisin Cookies • Chocolate Coconut and Pecan Cookies • Chocolate Coconut Macaroons • Chocolate Meringues • Chocolate Molasses Raisin Cookies • Classic Chocolate Chip Cookies • Coconut Chocolate Chip Cookies • Fudge Meringues • Ginger Chocolate Chip Cookies • Gluten-Free Chocolate Chip Cookies • Honey Chocolate Chip Cookies •

Maple Chocolate Chip Cookies • Nearly Nonfat Chocolate Cookies • Peppermint Chocolate Chip Cookies • Potato Chip Chocolate Chip Cookies • Pumpkin Chocolate Chip Cookies • Soft Chocolate Chip Oatmeal Cookies • Spumetti • Sweet Potato Chocolate Chip Cookies • Tofu Chocolate Chip Cookies • Triple Chocolate Chocolate Chip Cookies • White Chocolate Chocolate Chip Cookies

Chocolate
Cookies
A to Z

ALMOND COCONUT COOKIES

Early on, we decided that chocolate-dipped cookies were beyond the confines of this book. It seemed like cheating: you make a traditional cookie, dip it in melted chocolate, and call it a chocolate cookie. Great, no doubt—but is it truly a *chocolate* cookie? Our rule proved good until we wanted to come up with a cookie that was something of a cross between an Almond Joy and a Twix candy bar, two of our favorites. The long and short? Here's our one chocolate-dipped cookie—a crunchy almond-coconut wafer dipped in melted chocolate. Good enough to break every rule.

MAKES ABOUT 2 DOZEN COOKIES

1½	cups sweetened shredded coconut
½	cup plus 2 tablespoons sugar
½	teaspoon salt
10	tablespoons (1 stick plus 2 tablespoons) cool, unsalted butter, cut into small pieces
½	cup almond paste (4 ounces, see page 17)
2	large egg yolks, at room temperature
¼	teaspoon almond extract
2	cups all-purpose flour
12	ounces semisweet chocolate, chopped

1. Position the rack in the top third of the oven; preheat the oven to 350°F.

2. Spread the coconut on a large baking sheet and toast in the center of the oven until lightly browned and very fragrant, about 8 minutes, tossing quite often so that the coconut toasts evenly and doesn't burn. Transfer to a wire rack and cool completely. Maintain the oven's temperature.

3. Place the sugar and salt in a large bowl. (If you're using a stand mixer, do this step in the mixer's bowl.) Cut in the butter and almond paste with a pastry cutter or two forks, much as you would cut shortening into a piecrust dough, until the mixture resembles coarse meal.

4. Beat the mixture with an electric mixer at medium speed until softened, light, and evenly textured, if still a bit grainy, about 2 minutes. Beat in the egg yolks one at a time, then the almond extract until smooth. Finally, beat in the coconut just until evenly distributed. Remove the beaters, scraping off any batter that adheres to them.

5. Stir in the flour, using a wooden spoon or a rubber spatula, just until incorporated but not sticky. The dough will be firm, somewhat stiff—if your hands are clean, you can also work the flour in by hand without making the dough too stiff. Bring the dough together in a ball, then divide in half.

6. Lay a large sheet of plastic wrap or wax paper on a clean, dry work surface, then place one of the dough halves on top of it. Cover with a second large sheet of plastic wrap or wax paper. Use your palms and flattened fingers to press the dough into a ½-inch-thick circle, about 5 inches in diameter. Remove the top sheet of plastic wrap or wax paper, then trim the circle to a 4-inch square. Cut this square into rectangular sticks that are 4 inches long and ¾ inch wide. Transfer these sticks to a large, ungreased baking sheet, preferably nonstick, spacing them about 1 inch apart. Gather the scraps together and continue this process with the scraps and the other ball of dough, making more 4-inch by ¾-inch sticks, each ½ inch thick.

7. Bake in the top third of the oven for about 10 minutes until lightly browned and firm. Cool on the baking sheet for 1 minute, then transfer the cookies to a wire rack to cool completely. Cool the baking sheet for 5 minutes before baking additional batches.

8. When the cookies are cooled, place the chocolate in the top half of a double boiler set over about 2 inches of simmering water, or in a large bowl that fits very securely over a large pot with a similar amount of simmering water. Stir until less than half the chocolate has melted, then remove the double boiler's top half or the bowl from the heat. Be careful of escaping steam, which can burn your hands or condense in the chocolate and cause it to seize. Continue stirring off the heat until the chocolate has fully melted. Transfer the chocolate to a clean, dry, large bowl; cool for 5 minutes.

9. Lay a large sheet of wax paper on your work surface. Dip a cookie into the chocolate, coating one of its long sides, preferably the "bottom" side, the one that lays against the baking sheet. Gently scrape the cookie against the side of the bowl to create a thin, even layer of chocolate, then place the cookie, chocolate side down, on the wax paper. Continue with the remaining cookies.

10. When all the cookies have been dipped, use a pastry brush to paint the tops fairly heavily with melted chocolate, so that some of the chocolate drips over and coats the sides of the cookies. Let the coated cookies rest undisturbed until the chocolate coating sets, about 2 hours. It will help if you transfer them to a cool part of the house to set up.

Recommended storage
5 days at room temperature
3 months in the freezer (for best results, freeze the baked cookies,
then dip them in melted chocolate after defrosting)

Mix It Up!
Once the cookies have been dipped in chocolate, and before the chocolate hardens, sprinkle the tops with nonpareils (⅓ cup total volume), sliced almonds (½ cup), or toasted sweetened shredded coconut (½ cup).

To make pistachio coconut cookies, substitute ½ cup pistachio paste (4 ounces) for the almond paste. Once the cookies are dipped in chocolate, sprinkle ½ cup chopped pistachios over the tops of the cookies.

For a white chocolate or milk chocolate coating, omit the semisweet chocolate, substitute 12 ounces white chocolate or milk chocolate, and melt as directed.

BANANA CHOCOLATE CHIP COOKIES

little mashed banana replaces some of the butter in these sweet chocolate
chip cookies. The point here is taste, not a low-fat substitute; so use a very
ripe banana, one that's spotted brown, quite soft, and beyond the point where
you'd slice it onto cold cereal. These cookies are better the second day (if you can
wait that long), when that characteristic banana taste infuses them even more. Best
of all, they don't lose their crunch.

MAKES ABOUT 4 DOZEN COOKIES

2	cups all-purpose flour
½	cup rolled oats (do not use quick-cooking oats)
1	teaspoon baking soda
½	teaspoon salt
8	tablespoons (1 stick) cool, unsalted butter, cut into small pieces, plus additional for greasing the baking sheets
¼	cup solid vegetable shortening (2 ounces)
1	cup granulated sugar
½	cup packed light brown sugar
1	medium, very ripe banana, mashed (about ½ cup)
1	tablespoon vanilla extract
3	cups chocolate chips, preferably bittersweet chocolate chips

1. Position the rack in the center of the oven; preheat the oven to 350°F. Whisk the
flour, oats, baking soda, and salt in a medium bowl until uniform; set aside. Grease
a baking sheet with butter; set aside as well.

2. Beat the butter and shortening in a large bowl, using an electric mixer at
medium speed, until softened and of a uniform color, about 1 minute. Beat in both
sugars until fluffy but still a little grainy, about 1 more minute. Beat in the mashed
banana and vanilla. Remove the beaters.

3. Stir in the prepared flour mixture with a wooden spoon or rubber spatula until a soft, wet dough forms. Stir in the chocolate chips, just until evenly distributed.

4. Drop high, rounded teaspoonfuls of the dough onto the prepared baking sheet, spacing the mounds about 1½ inches apart.

5. Bake for about 12 minutes until bumpy and lightly browned. For best results, rotate the baking sheet back to front halfway through the baking process. Cool the cookies for 2 minutes on the baking sheet, then transfer to a wire rack to cool completely. Cool the baking sheet for 5 minutes before making additional batches.

> **Recommended storage**
> *4 days at room temperature*
> *3 months in the freezer*

More Choices!

Banana Cherry Chocolate Chip Cookies: Reduce the chocolate chips to 1½ cups; stir in 1½ cups dried cherries with the chips.

Banana Macadamia White Chocolate Chip Cookies: Substitute 1½ cups chopped unsalted macadamia nuts and 1½ cups white chocolate chips for the bittersweet chocolate chips.

Banana Nut Chocolate Chip Cookies: Reduce the chocolate chips to 1½ cups; add 1½ cups chopped walnuts or pecans with the chips.

Banana White Chocolate Chip Cookies: Substitute 3 cups white chocolate chips for the bittersweet chocolate chips.

Double Banana Chocolate Chip Cookies: Reduce the chocolate chips to 2 cups; stir in 1 cup crushed banana chips with the chips.

Tropical Chocolate Chip Cookies: Substitute rum extract for the vanilla extract. Reduce the chocolate chips to 1½ cups; add 1 cup chopped dried pineapple and ½ cup sweetened shredded coconut with the chips.

BIG SOFT CHOCOLATE COOKIES

Look no further for classic, bake-shop cookies like the ones you find in the big glass jars on the counter.

MAKES ABOUT 20 LARGE COOKIES

3	ounces unsweetened chocolate, chopped
2	cups all-purpose flour
½	teaspoon baking soda
¼	teaspoon salt
6	tablespoons cool, unsalted butter, cut into small pieces
¼	cup solid vegetable shortening (2 ounces)
1	cup packed dark brown sugar
¼	cup granulated sugar
1	large egg, at room temperature
1	teaspoon vanilla extract
¼	cup milk (regular or low-fat, but not nonfat)

1. Position the rack in the center of the oven. Preheat the oven to 350°F. Line a large baking sheet with parchment paper or a silicone baking mat; set aside.

2. Place the chocolate in the top of a double boiler set over about 1 inch of simmering water, placed over medium-high heat. If you don't have a double boiler, place the chocolate in a medium bowl that fits quite snugly over a medium saucepan with about 1 inch of simmering water in it. Stir with a heat-safe rubber spatula or a wooden spoon until half the chocolate has melted, then remove the top part of the double boiler or the bowl from the heat and continue stirring until all the chocolate has melted. Set aside to cool for 5 minutes.

3. Whisk the flour, baking soda, and salt in a medium bowl until uniform; set aside.

4. Beat the butter and shortening in a large bowl, using an electric mixer at medium speed, until softened and smooth, about 1 minute. Add the brown sugar and granulated sugar; continue beating at medium speed until pale brown, thick, but still somewhat grainy, about 2 more minutes. Beat in the egg and vanilla, then pour in the chocolate all at once and beat until smooth, about 1 minute at medium speed.

5. Using a wooden spoon or a rubber spatula, stir in half the prepared flour mixture just until you can see no white streaks in the batter. Stir in the milk until moderately smooth, then stir in the remainder of the flour just until uniform—there may still be small lumps in the soft, wet batter.

6. Drop by heaping tablespoonfuls onto the prepared baking sheet, spacing the mounds 2 inches apart. Bake for 16 minutes, rotating the sheet once during baking. When done, the cookies will have rounded, bumpy tops. Remove the baking sheet from the oven and press the cookies lightly with a heat-safe spatula or a large serving spoon, flattening them a tad to create smoother, rounded tops. Cool for 2 minutes on the baking sheet, then transfer the cookies to a wire rack to cool completely. Cool the baking sheet for 5 minutes before baking additional batches. Of course, you can also use more than one parchment-lined baking sheet, preparing one while the other bakes.

> **Recommended storage**
> *2 days at room temperature between sheets of wax paper*
> *1 month in the freezer*

Personalize It!

For an even fudgier consistency, bake the cookies 2 or 3 minutes less than the time recommended—beware: they will be very delicate, so you should let them cool on the baking sheet at least 5 minutes before transferring them to a wire rack.

These cookies are great for ice cream sandwiches. Let a 1-pint container soften about 5 minutes at room temperature, then place the container on its side and use a serrated knife to saw through the container, thereby making 1-inch-thick, perfectly round disks of ice cream. Peel off the container, place a disk on one cookie, top with a second, and enjoy!

BLACK BLACK AND WHITES

Purists, avert your eyes. Black and white cookies are nothing short of a New York City institution—you can find them everywhere from Carnegie Hall to Coney Island. Usually, they're a cakey, vanilla cookie, one half topped with vanilla icing and the other half with chocolate icing. Here we made the bottom cookie a soft chocolate cookie (naturally), then topped it the traditional way. It's not the custom of the country, but it may well start a trend.

MAKES ABOUT 16 LARGE COOKIES

FOR THE COOKIES

Nonstick spray

1¾	cups all-purpose flour
½	cup cocoa powder, sifted
½	teaspoon baking soda
¼	teaspoon salt
1	cup granulated sugar
½	cup solid vegetable shortening (4 ounces)
2	large eggs, at room temperature
½	cup milk (regular or low-fat, but not nonfat)
1	teaspoon vanilla extract

FOR THE ICING

1	ounce unsweetened chocolate, chopped
2½	cups confectioners' sugar, plus more as necessary
¼	cup water
1	tablespoon light corn syrup
1	teaspoon vanilla extract

1. To make the cookies, position the rack in the center of the oven; preheat the oven to 350°F. Spray a large baking sheet with nonstick spray; set aside. Whisk the flour, cocoa powder, baking soda, and salt in a medium bowl until a uniform color; set aside as well.

2. Beat the sugar and shortening in a large bowl until creamy, using an electric mixer at medium speed; continue beating until light and airy, about 1 minute.

3. Beat in the eggs one at a time, making sure the first is thoroughly incorporated before adding the second. Scrape down the sides of the bowl, then beat in the milk and vanilla until smooth.

4. Turn off the beaters, add the prepared flour mixture, then beat at low speed just until a smooth, moist dough forms, a little less than 1 minute.

5. Drop by heaping tablespoonfuls onto the prepared baking sheet, spacing the cookies about 3 inches apart. Use a dampened flatware tablespoon or a small rubber spatula to take the peaks off the mounds, flattening them slightly and creating fairly smooth tops.

6. Bake for 15 minutes, rotating the sheet once while baking. When done, the cookies should be lightly browned at the edges but somewhat soft. Cool for 2 minutes on the baking sheet, then transfer the cookies to a wire rack and cool completely before icing. Cool the baking sheet for 5 minutes before spraying again with nonstick spray and baking additional batches.

7. To make the icing, place the chocolate in the top part of a double boiler set over simmering water. Stir until half the chocolate has melted, then remove from the heat and continue stirring until all the chocolate has melted. Alternatively, place the chocolate in a small bowl and microwave on high for 20 seconds, stir, then continue heating in 15-second increments, stirring after each time, until almost all the chocolate has melted. Remove the bowl from the microwave oven and continue stirring until the chocolate has completely melted. Transfer the chocolate to a medium bowl and cool for 5 minutes. Meanwhile, place the confectioners' sugar in a large bowl; set aside.

8. Bring the water and corn syrup to a boil in a small saucepan, stirring once or twice to dissolve the corn syrup. The moment the mixture is at a full boil, pour it over the confectioners' sugar, then stir until smooth.

9. Pour half this sugar mixture into the bowl with the melted chocolate and stir until smooth.

10. Stir the vanilla into the remaining white icing mixture. Add more confectioners' sugar as necessary until the icing is thick, smooth, and spreadable, like a warm fondant icing.

11. Spread a large piece of wax paper under the wire cooling rack holding the cookies. Frost half of each cooled cookie with the chocolate icing, then the other half of each with the vanilla icing. It's best to place a small amount of icing on the cookie, then spread it with an offset spatula, but you can spread it with the back of a spoon, provided you wipe any icing off the spoon each time you use it. Place the iced cookies back on the wire rack so that any drips fall onto the wax paper. Leave undisturbed until the icing hardens, about 45 minutes.

Recommended storage
5 days at room temperature between sheets of wax paper
Not recommended for freezing

Customize It!

Because the cookie base is so classic in this recipe, the only real variations we recommend are with the icing. Here's a colorful assortment, all made by omitting the vanilla in step 10 (in the vanilla icing).

Black Black and Greens: Stir in ½ teaspoon mint extract and 2 drops green food coloring into the icing.

Black Black and Oranges: Stir in ½ teaspoon orange extract and 2 drops orange food coloring into the icing.

Black Black and Reds: Stir in ¼ teaspoon cherry flavoring and 2 drops red food coloring into the icing.

Black Black and Tans: Stir in ½ teaspoon almond extract and 1 drop brown or ivory food coloring into the icing.

Black Black and Yellows: Stir in ½ teaspoon lemon extract and 2 drops yellow food coloring into the icing.

BROWNIE DROPS

These intense chocolate treats taste like fudgy brownies, although they definitely have the texture of cookies. Soft and luscious, they will melt in your mouth. They're best warm, a few minutes out of the oven (if you can wait that long).

MAKES A LITTLE LESS THAN 4 DOZEN COOKIES

1	cup all-purpose flour
½	cup cocoa powder, sifted
½	teaspoon salt
¼	teaspoon baking soda
8	tablespoons (1 stick) unsalted butter, plus additional for greasing the baking sheets
2	ounces unsweetened chocolate, chopped
1	large egg, at room temperature
1	large egg white, at room temperature
1⅓	cups sugar
2	teaspoons vanilla extract

1. Position the racks in the top and bottom thirds of the oven; preheat the oven to 350°F.

2. Whisk the flour, cocoa powder, salt, and baking soda in a medium bowl until evenly colored; set aside. Butter two large baking sheets; set aside as well.

3. Cut the butter into small pieces, then place them and the chopped chocolate in the top half of a double boiler, set over a pot of lightly simmering water. If you don't have a double boiler, use a bowl that fits snugly over a saucepan of simmering water—but be careful of escaping steam, which can burn your hands. Stir the chocolate and butter until half the mixture has melted; remove the top part of the double boiler or the bowl from the pot and continue stirring away from the heat until all the chocolate and butter have melted. Transfer to a clean, medium bowl and cool for 5 minutes.

4. Beat the egg and egg white in a large bowl, using an electric mixer at low speed, until foamy. Raise the speed to medium and beat in the sugar, pouring it into the bowl in a slow, steady stream. Beat in the vanilla and continue beating until the sugar has mostly dissolved, about 2 minutes.

5. With the mixer running at low speed, pour in the melted chocolate mixture in a thin stream, stopping the mixer now and then so you can scrape down the sides of the bowl. Continue beating until all the melted chocolate and butter batter is a uniform, chocolaty brown.

6. Turn off the mixer, add the flour mixture all at once, then beat it in, first at low speed, then at medium speed. Continue beating until the dough gathers into a ball, about 1 minute. Do not mix by hand—rather, allow the mixture to establish the flour's glutens.

7. Take a heaping teaspoon of the dough and roll it into a ball between your hands, so that it's about the size of a small walnut. Place it on one of the prepared baking sheets, then continue rolling balls, spacing them about 1½ inches apart on the sheets (see Note). If you don't use up all your dough, cover the bowl loosely with a clean kitchen towel and let it sit at room temperature while you bake the first batch.

8. Bake for 5 minutes, then rotate the baking sheets top to bottom and back to front. Continue baking for about 6 more minutes until the cookies are puffed and lightly cracked. (The cookies will collapse a little as they cool.) Cool on the baking sheets for 5 minutes, then transfer the cookies to wire racks and cool completely. Cool the baking sheets for 5 minutes before buttering a second time and baking additional batches.

NOTE: *You can make these cookies in advance, rolling out the balls, placing them on the baking sheets, and then storing them in the refrigerator, covered, for up to 8 hours.*

Let the dough come back to room temperature before baking. This way, you can bake them right before you're ready to eat them—and they'll be at their warm, fudgy best.

Recommended storage
3 days at room temperature
3 months in the freezer

Customize It!

Add 1 cup of any of the following, or a combination, to the batter with the flour mixture: chocolate-covered espresso beans, chopped dried apricots, chopped dried figs, chopped hazelnuts, chopped pecans, chopped walnuts, cocoa nibs, dried cherries, M&M's, mini chocolate chips, Raisinets, raisins, Reese's Pieces, sliced almonds, sweetened shredded coconut.

BUTTERSCOTCH CHOCOLATE CHIP COOKIES

Be careful when you melt the butterscotch chips—the smallest amount of condensed steam can cause them to curdle. Because they're so temperamental, we don't advocate using a bowl over a pan of simmering water; use a double boiler or melt them in a microwave oven as indicated.

MAKES ABOUT 6 DOZEN COOKIES

2¼	cups plus 2 tablespoons all-purpose flour
1	teaspoon baking soda
1	teaspoon salt
8	tablespoons (1 stick) unsalted butter, plus additional for buttering the baking sheet
One	11-ounce package butterscotch chips
¾	cup packed light brown sugar
2	large eggs, at room temperature
1	teaspoon vanilla extract
3	cups semisweet or bittersweet chocolate chips

1. Position the rack in the center of the oven; preheat the oven to 350°F. Lightly butter a large baking sheet and set it aside. Whisk the flour, baking soda, and salt in a medium bowl; set aside as well.

2. Cut the butter into 1-inch pieces and place them with the butterscotch chips in the top half of a double boiler set over about 2 inches of simmering water. Stir constantly until about three-quarters melted, then remove from the heat and continue stirring until completely melted. Transfer the melted chips and butter to a large bowl and cool for 5 minutes. Alternatively, place the cut-up butter and butterscotch chips in a large bowl; microwave on high for 20 seconds, stir well, then continue heating on high in 15-second increments until about three-quarters melted. Remove the bowl from the microwave oven and continue stirring until completely melted. Set aside to cool for 5 minutes. (See Note.)

3. Beat the brown sugar into the melted butterscotch mixture, using an electric mixer at medium speed, for about 1 minute. Beat in the eggs one at a time, making sure the first is fully incorporated before adding the second. Scrape down the sides of the bowl and beat in the vanilla until smooth. Turn off the mixer, add the flour mixture, then beat at low speed just until soft, crumbly pieces of dough form, not until the mixture gathers into a ball. The dough will be quite thick and oily. Finally, beat in the chocolate chips at low speed, just until incorporated. You may also stir them in with a wooden spoon.

4. Roll by tablespoonfuls into 1-inch balls; place them on the prepared baking sheet, spacing them about 2 inches apart. Flatten each ball slightly with your fingers just until the sides begin to crack.

5. Bake for about 12 minutes. Use an oven mitt or a hot pad to hold on to the baking sheet, then give it two or three hard raps against the oven rack to make the cookies fall. Bake for about 1 more minute, or until the cookies are flat and crackly but somewhat soft to the touch. Cool on the baking sheet for 2 minutes, then transfer them to a wire rack to cool completely. Cool the baking sheet for 5 minutes, then lightly butter it again before baking further batches.

NOTE: *If the oil separates out of the melted butterscotch chips, all is not lost. The eggs, added later, will re-emulsify it as they're beaten in.*

Recommended storage
4 days at room temperature
3 months in the freezer

Mix It Up!
Banana Split Chocolate Chip Cookies: Reduce the chocolate chips to 1½ cups; add 1 cup crushed banana chips and ½ cup chopped dried strawberries with the remaining chips.

Butter Pecan Chocolate Chip Cookie: Reduce the chocolate chips to 1½ cups and add 1½ cups chopped pecans with the remaining chips.

Butterscotch Heath Bar Cookies: Omit the chocolate chips; substitute 3 cups chopped Heath bars.

Butterscotch Maple Chocolate Chip Cookies: Substitute maple extract for the vanilla extract.

Butterscotch Peanut Butter Chocolate Chip Cookies: Reduce the chocolate chips to 1½ cups and add 1½ cups peanut butter chips with the remaining chips.

Butterscotch Trail Mix Cookies: Substitute 3 cups purchased chocolate-chip trail mix for the chocolate chips.

CATS' TONGUES

Here's a chocolate version of one of the first French cookies, a favorite of professional bakers: *pailles d'or* (slivers of gold, a reference to their color) or more colloquially, *langues des chats* (cats' tongues, a reference to their elongated shape). We've taken these classic cookies and sandwiched them with a chocolate and raspberry filling.

MAKES ABOUT 2 DOZEN THIN SANDWICH COOKIES

3	large egg whites, at room temperature
1/8	teaspoon salt
6	tablespoons (3/4 stick) cool, unsalted butter, cut into small pieces, plus additional for greasing the baking sheet
1/2	cup sugar
1/2	cup plus 1 tablespoon all-purpose flour, plus additional for dusting the baking sheet
2	ounces semisweet chocolate, chopped
1 1/2	tablespoons raspberry liqueur, such as Chambord

1. Position the rack in the upper third of the oven only. Preheat the oven to 425°F. Butter and flour a large baking sheet; set aside. Beat the egg whites and salt in a small bowl with a fork until foamy; set aside as well.

2. Beat the butter in a large bowl, using an electric mixer at medium speed, until softened, about 1 minute. Add the sugar and beat until light and fluffy, about 1 more minute. Remove the beaters and use a rubber spatula to fold in the frothy egg-white mixture, adding one-quarter of it at a time. Continue folding and stirring until smooth and light. Finally, stir in the flour just until smooth and well incorporated.

3. Fit a pastry bag with a round, 3/8-inch tip; fill with the dough, squeezing it down toward the tip without compressing the dough tightly. Alternatively, place the dough in a zip-closed plastic bag and snip off one of the corners so that you have a 3/8-inch-wide opening.

4. Pipe or squeeze the dough onto the prepared baking sheet so that it forms fingerlike cookies about 3 inches in length. Space the cookies 2 inches apart.

5. Bake for about 6 minutes, or until the edges are a pale beige yet the middle is still springy to the touch. Cool on the baking sheet for 2 minutes, then transfer to a wire rack to cool completely. Cool the baking sheet for 5 minutes before buttering and flouring again so you can bake additional batches.

6. When all the cookies have cooled, place the chocolate in the top half of a double boiler set over about 1 inch of simmering water, or in a medium bowl that fits tightly over a medium saucepan with about the same amount of simmering water. Stir until half the chocolate has melted, then remove the double boiler's top half or the bowl from the heat and continue stirring until all the chocolate has melted. Cool for 10 minutes, then stir in the raspberry liqueur.

7. Brush the flat side of one of the cookies with about 1 teaspoon of the chocolate-raspberry mixture, then top with a second cookie, flat side down. Repeat with the remaining cookies to create all the sandwich cookies you can.

Recommended storage
3 days at room temperature between sheets of wax paper
If sandwiched, not recommended for freezing. The cookies alone can be
frozen for up to 2 months, then spread with the chocolate-raspberry filling
after thawing.

Customize It!
Rather than using semisweet chocolate and raspberry liqueur for the filling, substitute other combinations in equivalent amounts, such as bittersweet chocolate and Cognac, bittersweet chocolate and port, milk chocolate and Frangelico, semisweet chocolate and amaretto, semisweet chocolate and Original Canton Delicate Ginger Liqueur, semisweet chocolate and crème de banane, semisweet chocolate and Grand Marnier, white chocolate and crème de cacao, white chocolate and crème de menthe, white chocolate and Grand Marnier, or white chocolate and peach schnapps.

CHOCOLATE ALMOND HORNS

Traditional almond horns have no chocolate—perhaps for good reason, since it can cause them to spread and lose their characteristic crunchiness. But all is not lost for chocolate lovers. You can . . . well, have your horn and crunch it, too, provided you shave the chocolate and stir it into the batter without letting it melt. The chocolate taste is subtle but nonetheless satisfying.

MAKES 1 DOZEN LARGE, CRESCENT-SHAPED COOKIES

2	large egg whites, at room temperature
¼	teaspoon salt
One	7-ounce tube almond paste (see page 17)
⅓	cup sugar
1½	tablespoons all-purpose flour
1	teaspoon vanilla extract
1½	ounces semisweet chocolate, grated (see Chocolate grater, page 15)
¼	cup sliced almonds, roughly chopped

1. Position the rack in the center of the oven; preheat the oven to 350°F. Line a large baking sheet with parchment paper or a silicone baking mat; set aside. Beat the egg whites and salt in a small bowl with a fork until frothy; set aside.

2. Cut the almond paste into the sugar in a large bowl, using a pastry cutter or two forks; continue working until the mixture resembles coarse meal. (If you're using a stand mixer, do this in the mixer's bowl.) Beat in the flour and vanilla with an electric mixer at medium speed until smooth, a little less than 1 minute.

3. Remove 1 tablespoon from the frothy beaten egg whites and place it in a second small bowl, reserving it for later in the recipe. With the beaters running at low speed, pour half the remaining egg-white mixture into the batter in a thin stream. Continue beating until smooth. Then beat in the remainder of the egg-white mixture in 2-teaspoon increments until the mixture is thick and pasty, too wet to roll out but not as wet as icing, about like sticky peanut butter. You'll probably have

1 or 2 teaspoons of beaten egg white left over; add this to the reserved amount of egg whites and set that aside again. Slowly and gently, stir the grated chocolate into the batter.

4. Fit a pastry bag with a round, ¾-inch tip and fill the bag with the wet dough, squeezing it down toward the tip. Pipe the dough out onto the prepared baking sheet, making a curved, crescent-shaped horn about 5 inches long. Continue making these horns, spacing them about 1½ inches apart. Brush them lightly with the reserved egg-white mixture, then sprinkle with the chopped almonds.

5. Bake for 16 to 20 minutes, or until the cookies are lightly browned and firm to the touch. Cool the cookies completely on the baking sheet before removing them for storage.

Recommended storage
4 days at room temperature
2 months in the freezer

Personalize It!

Any changes to the batter will dramatically affect the delicate texture of these classics. We recommend dipping the cooled cookies in 6 ounces of white, semisweet, or bittersweet chocolate that has been melted and cooled for 5 minutes.

Before the chocolate shell hardens, you can coat the dipped cookies by sprinkling chopped whole almonds, sliced almonds, or slivered almonds over their tops (you'll need ⅓ cup total volume).

CHOCOLATE BISCOTTI

Look no further for the ultimate dunking cookies. These are Italian classics, baked twice so they'll stand up to every beverage, from red wine to hot chocolate. Don't slice the cookies too thin after the first baking—they need to be somewhat thick so they can dry out without falling apart during the second go-round in the oven.

MAKES ABOUT 2 DOZEN COOKIES

2½ cups all-purpose flour, plus additional for dusting the work surface
4 ounces semisweet chocolate, chopped
¼ cup plus 2 tablespoons cocoa powder, sifted
1 teaspoon baking powder
½ teaspoon baking soda
¼ teaspoon salt
3 large eggs, at room temperature
1 cup sugar
2 tablespoons unsalted butter, melted and cooled
1 tablespoon vanilla extract

1. Position the rack in the center of the oven. Preheat the oven to 325°F. Line a large baking sheet with parchment paper or a silicone baking mat; set aside.

2. Place ½ cup of the flour and the chopped chocolate in a food processor or a mini food processor fitted with the chopping blade. Pulse a few times, then process until powdery, but not until the fat in the chocolate liquefies and the mixture becomes a paste. Transfer this chocolate powder to a medium bowl and whisk in the remaining 2 cups flour, cocoa powder, baking powder, baking soda, and salt until uniformly colored. Set aside.

3. Beat the eggs and sugar in a large bowl, using an electric mixer at medium speed, until satiny, thick, and pale yellow, about 2 minutes. Scrape down the sides of the bowl and beat in the melted butter and vanilla until smooth. Turn off the beaters, add the flour mixture, and then beat at low speed just until a crumbly but still moist dough forms.

4. Lightly dust a clean, dry work surface with flour. Turn the dough out and knead 10 or 12 times to get it to cohere into a single mass. Divide in half and form each into a log about 6 inches long. Flatten each log into an oval cylinder about 1½ inches high at its apex. Transfer the logs to the prepared baking sheet.

5. Bake for about 45 minutes, or until the tops are cracked and dry. Cool on the baking sheet until the logs are easily handled, about 30 minutes. Maintain the oven's temperature.

6. Transfer the logs to a cutting board and slice into ½-inch thick cookies. If you slice on the diagonal, you'll have longer cookies; a serrated knife will work best to keep the dough from crumbling. Transfer the cut cookies to the baking sheet, still lined with parchment or a silicone baking mat, placing them, cut side down, about ¼ inch apart.

7. Bake for another 10 minutes, then turn the cookies over to the other cut side and bake for about 10 more minutes, or until firm and lightly toasted. Transfer the cookies to a wire rack to cool completely. (Do not cool the cookies on the baking sheet or they will steam and lose their crunch.)

> *Recommended storage*
> *1 week at room temperature*
> *3 months in the freezer once baked*

Dipped Biscotti

Place 12 ounces bittersweet, semisweet, milk, or white chocolate in the top half of a double boiler set over simmering water, or a medium bowl set over a saucepan with a small amount of simmering water; stir until half the chocolate has melted, then remove from the heat and continue stirring until all the chocolate has melted. Cool for 5 minutes. Dip the cooled biscotti into the chocolate, then place the cookies on a wire rack set over wax paper for about 30 minutes until

the chocolate coating hardens.

Before the coating hardens, you can sprinkle ½ cup chopped crystallized ginger, chopped pecans, chopped pistachios, crushed Heath bars, nonpareils, or sliced almonds over the cookies.

CHOCOLATE CARAMEL POCKETS

These cakey cookies are like tender chocolate pillows, each stuffed with a caramel. They are best eaten moments out of the oven as the caramels will become firm after a few hours. The taste will be the same, but the luxuriously soft texture of the warm cookies will be somewhat compromised. So plan to make these as a time-out while your kids are playing a game, or while your spouse is watching one.

MAKES ABOUT 3 DOZEN COOKIES

36	chewy caramel cube candies
2¼	cups all-purpose flour
½	cup cocoa powder, sifted
½	teaspoon baking powder
¼	teaspoon salt
½	pound (2 sticks) cool, unsalted butter, cut into small pieces
½	cup granulated sugar
½	cup packed dark brown sugar
1	large egg, at room temperature
1	large egg yolk, at room temperature
2	teaspoons vanilla extract

1. Position the rack in the center of the oven; preheat the oven to 350°F. Cut each of the caramels in half; set them aside. Whisk the flour, cocoa powder, baking powder, and salt in a medium bowl until uniformly colored; set aside as well.

2. Beat the butter in a large bowl, using an electric mixer, until softened and somewhat smooth, about 1 minute. Add both kinds of sugar and continue beating at medium speed until light and fluffy, about 1 minute. Beat in the egg and egg yolk, then the vanilla, until smooth, about 30 seconds. Stop the mixer, pour in the prepared flour mixture, then beat at low speed just until a soft, pliable dough forms.

3. Scoop up 1 tablespoon of the dough, set it in your palm, and flatten it slightly into a squat, puffy disk; set two caramel halves side by side in the middle of this disk. Wrap the sides of the disk over the caramels, taking care not to smush them together—then continue pushing the cookie together until you can seal it into a squat ball, like a tiny deflated basketball. Place this on a large, ungreased baking sheet, preferably a nonstick sheet. Continue making these stuffed cookies, spacing them about 1½ inches apart.

4. Bake for about 12 minutes, or until the dough is set but still slightly springy to the touch. Cool the cookies on the sheet for 2 minutes, then transfer them to a wire rack to cool completely. Cool the baking sheet for 5 minutes before baking additional cookies on it.

Recommended storage
3 days at room temperature
Not recommended for freezing

More Choices!

Chocolate Almond Pockets: Substitute 36 chocolate-covered almonds for the caramels; do not cut the almonds in half.

Chocolate Cherry Pockets: Substitute 36 candied cherries for the caramels; do not cut the cherries in half.

Chocolate Chestnut Pockets: Substitute 18 marrons glacées (candied chestnuts) for the caramels; cut the marrons glacées in half and wrap one half inside each cookie before baking.

Chocolate Hazelnut Pockets: Substitute 36 whole hazelnuts for the caramels; do not cut the hazelnuts in half.

Chocolate Kiss Pockets: Substitute 36 Hershey's Kisses for the caramels; do not cut the Kisses in half.

CHOCOLATE CHEWS

T hink of these delicate cookies as fallen meringues: very moist inside, crunchy outside. Make sure the sliced almonds are fresh—they should smell sweet and nutty, not tangy or sharp. If you buy them in bulk, store them in the freezer for up to two months and don't thaw them before you use them.

MAKES ABOUT 3 DOZEN SMALL, MERINGUE-LIKE COOKIES

1	cup all-purpose flour
1	teaspoon baking soda
½	teaspoon salt
2	ounces unsweetened chocolate, chopped
½	cup sliced almonds
1⅓	cups packed dark brown sugar
2	large eggs, at room temperature
1	teaspoon vanilla extract

1. Position the rack in the center of the oven; preheat the oven to 350°F. Line two large baking sheets with parchment paper or a silicone baking mat; set aside. Whisk the flour, baking soda, and salt in a medium bowl until uniform; set aside as well.

2. Place the chocolate in the top half of a double boiler set over about 1 inch of simmering water, or in a medium bowl that fits snugly over a medium saucepan with a similar amount of simmering water. Stir until half the chocolate has melted, then remove the double boiler's top part or the bowl from the heat and continue stirring until the chocolate has completely melted. Alternatively, place the chopped chocolate in a medium bowl and microwave on high for 20 seconds, stir, then continue heating in 15-second increments on high, stirring after each one. When about two-thirds of the chocolate has melted, remove it from the microwave oven and continue stirring until it's all melted. In all cases, transfer the chocolate to a small bowl and set it aside to cool for 5 minutes.

3. Spread the almonds on a third baking sheet or in a small, shallow roasting pan. Toast them in the oven for about 5 minutes, stirring once or twice, until lightly browned and very fragrant. Set aside to cool for 5 minutes as well.

4. Beat the brown sugar and eggs in a large bowl with an electric mixer at medium speed until thick, satiny, and pale brown, about 2 minutes. Pour in the cool chocolate in a slow, steady stream, beating all the while. Scrape down the sides of the bowl, then beat in the vanilla until smooth. Remove the beaters and stir in the prepared flour mixture with a wooden spoon or a rubber spatula just until moistened. Finally, stir in the toasted almond until evenly distributed.

5. Drop by heaping teaspoonfuls onto one of the prepared baking sheets, spacing the mounds about 2 inches apart. Bake for 10 minutes, or until the tops are slightly cracked but the cookies are still soft inside. Cool completely on the baking sheet before removing the cookies from the parchment paper. Meanwhile, bake a second batch on the second prepared baking sheet, as directed.

> **Recommended storage**
> *2 days at room temperature between sheets of wax paper*
> *Not recommended for freezing*

Personalize It!

Chocolate Cranberry Chews: Stir in ½ cup dried cranberries with the toasted almonds.

Chocolate Ginger Chews: Stir in ½ cup finely chopped crystallized ginger with the toasted almonds.

Chocolate Peanut Chews: Substitute ½ cup finely chopped, unsalted, roasted peanuts for the almonds. Omit toasting the peanuts.

Chocolate Pecan Chews: Substitute ½ cup finely chopped pecans for the almonds. Toast only 3 or 4 minutes.

Chocolate Walnut Chews: Substitute ½ cup finely chopped walnuts for the almonds. Toast only 3 or 4 minutes.

CHOCOLATE CHIP BISCOTTI

There's nothing so good as crunchy biscotti, dunked in coffee, vin santo, or even that bit of red wine left at the end of dinner. Don't shortchange the baking times here—you want the cookies to dry out and become quite hard.

MAKES ABOUT 2 DOZEN BISCOTTI

2	cups plus 1 tablespoon all-purpose flour, plus additional for dusting the work surface
1	teaspoon baking soda
½	teaspoon salt
1½	cups semisweet mini chocolate chips
3	tablespoons cool, unsalted butter, cut into small pieces
¾	cup sugar
1	cup sliced almonds
2	large eggs, at room temperature
2	large egg whites, at room temperature
1	teaspoon vanilla extract

1. Position the rack in the center of the oven; preheat the oven to 350°F. Line a large baking sheet with parchment paper or a silicone baking mat; set aside. Mix 2 cups flour, the baking soda, and salt in a medium bowl; set aside. In a second medium bowl, mix the mini chocolate chips with the remaining 1 tablespoon flour, coating them thoroughly; set aside as well.

2. Soften the butter in a large bowl, using an electric mixer at medium speed. Add the sugar and continue beating until grainy but incorporated, about 1 minute. Beat in the sliced almonds with the mixer to crush them up into the batter. Add both the eggs and continue beating until smooth, then add the egg whites and vanilla, beating at medium speed until the dough is light and uniform, about 1 more minute.

3. Turn off the mixer, add the flour mixture, then mix in at lowest speed possible, just until no flour is visible in the batter. Do not beat until the dough gathers into a ball. Remove the beaters and fold in the flour-coated chips with a wooden spoon or a rubber spatula just until evenly distributed.

4. Dust a clean, dry work surface with flour, then turn the dough out onto it. Dust your hands with flour, then knead the dough lightly until silky, about 2 minutes. Cut the dough in half and make two logs, each about 9 inches long. Flatten the logs slightly into oval cylinders about 1½ inches high, then place them 4 inches apart on the prepared baking sheet.

5. Bake for about 40 minutes, or until the logs are set, dry, and firm to the touch. There should be some small fissures in the logs; they should also be browned slightly at the tops and along the edges. Cool on the baking sheet for 20 minutes. Meanwhile, reduce the oven temperature to 300°F.

6. Transfer the logs to your work surface and use a serrated knife to slice into cookies about ¾ inch thick. If desired, slice at a diagonal, rather than straight across the log, thereby making longer cookies. Place these cookies cut side down on a large baking sheet spacing them ½ inch apart. You may need to use more than one baking sheet, lined with a second sheet of parchment paper or baking mat.

7. Bake for about 8 minutes, then turn each cookie over and continue baking for about 10 more minutes, or until dry, crisp, and lightly toasted. Cool on the baking sheet for 2 minutes, then transfer to a wire rack and cool completely.

Recommended storage
1 week at room temperature
3 months in the freezer

More Choices

Cocoa Nib Biscotti: Substitute cocoa nibs for the mini chocolate chips.

Currant Chocolate Chip Biscotti: Reduce the mini chocolate chips to 1 cup; add ½ cup dried currants with the remaining chocolate chips.

Orange Chocolate Chip Biscotti: Add ½ teaspoon orange extract and 1 tablespoon finely grated orange zest with the chocolate chips.

CHOCOLATE CHIP MERINGUES

These small meringues are made with mini chocolate chips. You can also chop regular chocolate chips to about half their size for similar results. To get the best height from your egg whites, make sure they're fresh and at room temperature, don't get a single speck of yolk in the whites, and make sure the bowl is thoroughly dry and at room temperature. To freeze the yolks for a later use, whisk them lightly with a pinch of salt to prevent coagulation while frozen.

MAKES SLIGHTLY LESS THAN 4 DOZEN MERINGUES

4	large egg whites, at room temperature
¼	teaspoon salt
¼	teaspoon cream of tartar
1	cup sugar
1	teaspoon vanilla extract
2	cups mini chocolate chips

1. Position the racks in the top and bottom thirds of the oven. Preheat the oven to 225°F. Line two large baking sheets with parchment paper or silicone baking mats.

2. Beat the egg whites and salt in a large bowl with an electric mixer at medium speed until frothy; then add the cream of tartar, increase the mixer's speed to high, and beat until soft peaks form. Beat in the sugar in 1-tablespoon increments, pouring it slowly in as the beaters whir. You may need to scrape down the sides of the bowl occasionally—make sure your spatula is dry, without a drop of water on it. Add the vanilla and continue beating for about 6 minutes, or until you can't feel any grains of sugar when you rub a small amount between your fingers. Stir in the mini chocolate chips with a wooden spoon or a rubber spatula.

3. Drop by tablespoonfuls onto the prepared baking sheets, spacing the meringues about 1 inch apart. Bake for 1½ hours, rotating the sheets top to bottom and back to front after 45 minutes. When done, the meringues should be quite dry and very firm to the touch—you should be able to lift one easily off the sheet. Let them cool completely on the sheets before removing them.

Make It Your Own!

Almond Chocolate Chip Meringues: Substitute ½ teaspoon almond extract for the vanilla extract; reduce the chocolate chips to 1 cup and stir in 1 cup sliced almonds with the remaining chips.

Mint Chocolate Chip Meringues: Omit the vanilla extract; beat in ½ teaspoon mint extract and 3 drops green food coloring in place of the vanilla.

Pecan Chocolate Chip Meringues: Reduce the chocolate chips to 1 cup; add 1 cup chopped pecans with the remaining chips.

Walnut Chocolate Chip Meringues: Reduce the chocolate chips to 1 cup; add 1 cup chopped walnuts with the remaining chips.

CHOCOLATE CHIP OATMEAL COOKIES

Of all our cookies, these look most like packaged, store-bought chocolate chip cookies. They're crunchy on the outside but cakey inside, thanks to the oatmeal and increased baking soda. One thing we guarantee: these are loaded with more chips than any store-bought cookie you've had in a long time.

MAKES ABOUT 4 DOZEN

2¼	cups rolled oats (do not use quick-cooking oats)
1¼	cups all-purpose flour
1	teaspoon baking soda
1	teaspoon salt
8	tablespoons (1 stick) cool, unsalted butter, cut into small pieces, plus additional for greasing the baking sheets
½	cup solid vegetable shortening (4 ounces)
1	cup granulated sugar
½	cup packed light brown sugar
1	large egg, at room temperature
2	teaspoons vanilla extract
3	cups semisweet or bittersweet chocolate chips

1. Position the racks in the top and bottom thirds of the oven; preheat the oven to 375°F. Lightly butter two large baking sheets; set aside. Whisk the oats, flour, baking soda, and salt in a medium bowl until well combined; set aside.

2. Beat the butter and shortening in a large bowl, using an electric mixer at medium speed, until softened and somewhat creamy, about 1 minute. Add both sugars and continue beating until airy, pale yellowy-brown, but still a little grainy, about 2 minutes. Beat in the egg and vanilla all at once.

3. Turn the mixer off, pour in the oat and flour mixture, then beat at very low speed just until incorporated. The dough should be cohesive but crumbly. Remove the beaters, scrape any dough on them back into the batter, and stir in the chocolate chips with a wooden spoon or rubber spatula until distributed throughout.

4. Roll the dough into balls about the size of a walnut and place on the prepared baking sheets, spacing them about 1½ inches apart. Flatten the balls slightly with the back of a flatware spoon—don't make an indentation or let the sides crack; rather, gently push down, just to take the roundness off the tops.

5. Bake for 8 minutes, then rotate the sheets back to front and top to bottom. Continue baking for about 8 more minutes, or until the cookies are lightly browned but still soft to the touch. Cool for 3 minutes on the sheets, then transfer the cookies to wire racks and cool completely. Cool the baking sheets for 5 minutes, then butter them again to make additional batches.

Recommended storage
4 days at room temperature
3 months in the freezer

Customize It!
Substitute an equivalent amount of M&M's, mint chocolate chips. Reese's Pieces, or white chocolate chips for the semisweet chocolate chips.

Reduce the chocolate chips to 2 cups and add 1 cup of any of the following with the remaining chocolate chips: butterscotch chips; chopped dried pears; chopped hazelnuts, pecans, or walnuts; dried cherries; dried cranberries; finely chopped dried apricots; peanut butter chips; or raisins.

Add one of the following with the vanilla extract: 1 teaspoon banana extract, 2 teaspoons finely grated lemon zest, 1 teaspoon maple extract, or 1 teaspoon rum extract.

CHOCOLATE CHOCOLATE CHIP COOKIES

Loaded with chocolate, these dense little cookies are just short of divine. For chocoholics, they may be pure heaven.

MAKES ABOUT 4 DOZEN COOKIES

1	cup all-purpose flour
⅓	cup cocoa powder, sifted
½	teaspoon salt
6	ounces semisweet chocolate, chopped
14	tablespoons (1 stick plus 6 tablespoons) cool, unsalted butter, cut into small pieces
1½	cups sugar
2	large eggs, at room temperature
1	tablespoon vanilla extract
3	cups bittersweet chocolate chips (preferably), or semisweet chocolate chips

1. Position the racks in the top and bottom thirds of the oven; preheat the oven to 375°F. Whisk the flour, cocoa powder, and salt in a medium bowl until uniformly colored; set aside.

2. Place the chocolate in the top half of a double boiler set over about 2 inches of simmering water. If you don't have a double boiler, place the chocolate in a bowl that fits snugly over a medium saucepan with about the same amount of simmering water. Adjusting the heat to prevent a furious boil, stir until half the chocolate has melted; remove the top half of the double boiler or the bowl from the heat—but be careful of escaping steam. Continue stirring off the heat until all the chocolate has melted. Transfer to a clean, dry bowl and cool for 5 minutes. (Transferring the chocolate will keep it from cooking against the still-warm sides of the double boiler's top or the heated bowl.)

3. Meanwhile, soften the butter in a large bowl, using an electric mixer at medium speed. Add the sugar and beat until fluffy and pale yellow but still grainy, about 1 minute. Beat in the eggs one at a time, making sure the first is thoroughly incorporated before adding the second. Beat in the vanilla, then the cooled, melted chocolate just until the batter looks smooth and uniform. Turn the mixer off, add the prepared flour mixture, and beat at low speed just until incorporated. The batter will be like thick buttercream frosting. Fold in the chips, either with the mixer at low speed or with a rubber spatula.

4. Drop by tablespoonfuls onto two large, ungreased baking sheets, preferably nonstick, spacing the cookies about 1½ inches apart. Bake for 7 minutes, then rotate the sheets top to bottom and back to front. Continue baking for 6 to 8 more minutes, until the cookies are puffed but firm and set—if you lightly touch one, you should not make an indent. Cool on the sheets for 5 minutes, then transfer the cookies to wire racks to cool completely. Cool the baking sheets for 5 minutes before proceeding with additional batches.

> **Recommended storage**
> *5 days at room temperature*
> *3 months in the freezer*

Customize It!

Reduce the chocolate chips to 1½ cups and add 1½ cups of any, or any combination, of the following to the batter with the remaining chocolate chips: chocolate-covered espresso beans, chopped dried apricots, chopped dried figs, chopped hazelnuts, chopped pecans, chopped walnuts, dried cherries, golden raisins, pine nuts, unsalted sunflower seeds, or toasted pepitas.

Omit the chocolate chips entirely and substitute 3 cups of any of the following: butterscotch chips, M&M's Mini Baking Bits, mint chocolate chips, peanut butter chips, or white chocolate chips.

For cakier cookies in the base recipe or any variation, stir ½ teaspoon baking soda into the flour mixture before adding it to the batter.

CHOCOLATE CHUNK COOKIES

Fans of chunk cookies, look no further. Here's a slightly chewy cookie, soft and moist so it can hold up against all the irregular chocolate pieces in the batter. If you want more crunch, enjoy them the next day, when they've had a chance to dry out slightly on the outside while remaining soft inside.

MAKES ABOUT 4 DOZEN COOKIES

3	cups all-purpose flour
½	teaspoon baking soda
½	teaspoon cream of tartar
½	teaspoon salt
½	pound (2 sticks) cold, unsalted butter, cut into small pieces
1⅓	cups packed dark brown sugar
¼	cup granulated sugar
2	tablespoons light corn syrup
1	large egg, at room temperature
2	large egg whites, at room temperature
1	teaspoon vanilla extract
3	cups chocolate chunks (see Note)

1. Position the racks in the top and bottom thirds of the oven; preheat the oven to 375°F. Whisk the flour, baking soda, cream of tartar, and salt in a medium bowl until uniform; set aside.

2. Beat the butter, brown sugar, and granulated sugar in a large bowl, using an electric mixer at medium speed, until soft, light, but still a bit grainy, about 1 minute. Beat in the corn syrup, then beat in the egg, egg whites, and vanilla until uniform, fluffy, and a little runny, a little less than 1 minute.

3. Turn off the mixer, add the flour mixture, then beat at low speed just until a meltingly soft batter forms, about 30 seconds. Do not overbeat—its color should not lighten much at this point—and do not allow the dough to become glutinous.

Stir in the chocolate chunks with a wooden spoon, then drop the batter by table-spoonfuls onto two large, ungreased baking sheets, preferably nonstick, spacing the cookies about 3 inches apart.

4. Bake for 6 minutes, then rotate the sheets top to bottom and back to front. Continue baking for about 6 more minutes, or until the cookies have spread and started to brown at the edges. They should still be quite soft, even a little gooey, but stabilized, not wet and raw. Cool on the sheets for 5 minutes—they will become mushy if removed too soon—then gently transfer them with a metal spatula to wire racks to cool completely. Cool the baking sheets for 5 minutes before making additional batches, as necessary.

NOTE: *You can purchase chocolate chunks in most supermarkets and almost all gourmet markets. To make your own, use a chef's knife to cut dark chocolate bars into uniform chunks.*

Recommended storage
4 days at room temperature between sheets of wax paper
2 months in the freezer

Personalize It!
Reduce the chocolate chips to 1½ cups; add 1½ cups of any of the following: chopped dried figs, chopped walnut pieces, cocoa nibs, dried cherries, dried cranberries, M&M's, pecan pieces, raisins, Reese's Pieces, unsalted roasted peanuts, or white chocolate chunks.

CHOCOLATE CINNAMON CHECKERBOARDS

These intricate, beautiful cookies look like small checkerboards. Admittedly, they're a bit of work—you'll need to make two doughs, weave them into a checkerboard pattern, then cut them into rectangular cookies. But the results are worth the extra effort: a crunchy, light, spiced cookie that's sure to be a hit at every party, potluck, or family gathering.

MAKES ABOUT 3 DOZEN SMALL, RECTANGULAR COOKIES

2	ounces unsweetened chocolate, chopped
1⅔	cups all-purpose flour, plus additional for dusting
¼	teaspoon baking powder
¼	teaspoon salt
8	tablespoons (1 stick) cool, unsalted butter, cut into small pieces
6	tablespoons solid vegetable shortening (3 ounces)
1	cup plus 2 tablespoons confectioners' sugar
4	large egg yolks, at room temperature
2	teaspoons vanilla extract
¼	cup granulated sugar
2	tablespoons ground cinnamon

1. Place the chocolate in the top half of a double boiler set over a pot of simmering water, or in a medium bowl that fits tightly over a medium saucepan of simmering water. Stir until half the chocolate has melted, then remove the top half of the double boiler or the bowl from the heat and continue stirring until all the chocolate has melted. You can also melt the chocolate in the microwave oven by placing it in a medium bowl and microwaving it on high for 20 seconds, stirring well, then continuing to heat on high in 15-second increments, stirring after each heating; when about two-thirds of the chocolate has melted, continue stirring outside the microwave oven until all has melted. Transfer the melted chocolate to a clean, dry bowl and set aside to cool for 5 minutes.

2. Whisk the flour, baking powder, and salt in a medium bowl until well combined; set aside.

3. Soften the butter and shortening in a large bowl, using an electric mixer at medium speed; add the confectioners' sugar and continue beating (on low at first, then at medium speed) until light and fluffy, about 1 minute. Beat in one egg yolk at a time, making sure each is thoroughly incorporated before adding the next. Beat in the vanilla. Remove the beaters and stir in the prepared flour mixture with a wooden spoon or a rubber spatula just until moistened. Gather the dough together into a ball.

4. Divide the ball of dough in half. You need a very precise reading of half for this recipe, so we suggest using kitchen scales to get an accurate measurement. If you don't have a kitchen scale, scoop out the dough in ¼-cup increments, going back and forth between two clean bowls until you're sure you have half in each bowl. Stir the melted, cooled chocolate into one of the halves of the dough. (You may find it works best to use your hands.) Wrap each half in plastic wrap, flatten into thick disks, and refrigerate until firm but not rock hard, about 1 hour but not more than 3 hours.

5. Position the rack in the center of the oven; preheat the oven to 375°F. Line a large baking sheet with parchment paper or a silicone baking mat; set aside. Combine the granulated sugar and cinnamon on a large plate; set aside as well.

6. Unwrap the two sections of dough (one vanilla and one chocolate) and place them each on a lightly floured, dry surface. Dust each section of dough with flour, then roll or press each into an 8-inch circle, about ½ inch thick. Place the chocolate circle on top of the vanilla one; press very lightly to adhere. (The stacked dough is about 1 inch thick and you don't want to lose its height or shape by pressing too hard.) Use a ruler to help you trim the circles into a 6-inch square. Set the trimmings aside for another use—see below for one idea.

7. Cut the square in half, then separate the halves somewhat. Cut each half into 3 long, 1-inch-wide strips. Flip the center strip in each half, thereby reversing the chocolate/vanilla combination in the middle of each of the 3-strip sections. Square up the edges of each half with a ruler or a dough scraper (in case the halves have bulged out while being cut), then press down again very lightly. Do not flatten—the point is to make sure the cookie strips are adhering to each other.

8. Dip one of these 3-strip blocks into the prepared sugar and cinnamon mixture on the plate, coating the top, bottom, and long sides, not the checkerboard ends. Return it to your work surface and slice it off into cookies slightly less than ½ inch thick, cutting across the stripes, or at a 90-degree angle to the strips on the top of the block (thinner slices produce crunchier cookies; thicker ones, cakier cookies). The cookies sliced off the block will be rectangles of about 1 × 3 inches. Place the cookies, cut side down, on the prepared baking sheet, spacing them about 1 inch apart.

9. Bake for 15 minutes, reversing the sheet front to back halfway through the baking process. The cookies should be lightly browned but still springy to the touch. Cool for 2 minutes on the baking sheet, then transfer the cookies to a wire rack to cool completely. Cool the baking sheet for 5 minutes (or use a second baking sheet lined with parchment paper or a silicone baking mat), then continue slicing and baking the remainder of the cookies.

Recommended storage
3 days at room temperature
2 months in the freezer

Suggestions for the Trimmings:

Combine the reserved trimmings into one ball. Roll out this dough on a lightly floured surface, then cut out 3-inch round cookies or any shape cookies, using a similarly sized cutter for marbleized cookies. Bake on a cookie sheet lined with parchment paper or a silicone baking mat for about 15 minutes at 350°F.

Pinch off sections of dough and roll them into balls about the size of a walnut. Roll these small balls in a mixture of 2 teaspoons cinnamon and 2 tablespoons sugar similar to the one in the base recipe. Flatten slightly with a fork, making a cross-hatch pattern. Place on a baking sheet lined with parchment paper or a silicone baking mat. Bake at 375°F for about 15 minutes, or until set but still somewhat soft.

CHOCOLATE COCONUT AND PECAN COOKIES

These classic "sandy" cookies are crisp, chewy, and full of chocolate flavor. It doesn't get much easier—or better—than this. You don't have to toast the pecans (they'll toast right in the cookie as they bake), and you don't have to do anything fancy to the dough. In fact, we think of these cookies as a lunchbox favorite: they travel well because they're not too soft, not too crumbly, and stay moist for a long time.

MAKES ABOUT 3 DOZEN COOKIES

1½	cups all-purpose flour
½	teaspoon baking soda
¼	teaspoon salt
3	ounces unsweetened chocolate, chopped
6	tablespoons (¾ stick) cool, unsalted butter, cut into small pieces
1	cup plus 2 tablespoons sugar
3	large eggs, at room temperature
1½	teaspoons vanilla extract
1	cup sweetened shredded coconut
¾	cup chopped pecan pieces

1. Position the racks in the top and bottom thirds of the oven; preheat the oven to 375°F. Line two large baking sheets with parchment paper or silicone baking mats; set aside. Whisk the flour, baking soda, and salt in a medium bowl until well combined; set aside as well.

2. Place the chopped chocolate in the top half of a double boiler set over about 1 inch of simmering water, or in a medium bowl that fits tightly over a medium saucepan with about the same amount of simmering water. Stir until half the chocolate has melted, then remove the double boiler's top half or the bowl from the heat and continue stirring until all the chocolate has melted. Cool for 5 minutes.

3. Meanwhile, soften the butter in a large bowl, using an electric mixer at medium speed, about 1 minute. Add the sugar and continue beating until light and fluffy but still somewhat grainy, about 1 more minute. Beat in the eggs one at a time, making sure each is thoroughly incorporated before adding the next. Beat in the vanilla extract, then the cooled, melted chocolate until it looks smooth (if you rub it between your fingers, you may still feel grains of sugar). Turn off the beaters, add the prepared flour mixture, then beat at a very low speed until a soft, pliable dough forms. Let the mixer beat in the coconut and pecans at a very low speed, just until evenly distributed.

4. Drop by rounded tablespoonfuls onto the prepared baking sheets, spacing the drops about 2 inches apart. Bake for 7 minutes, then reverse the sheets top to bottom and back to front. Continue baking for about 6 more minutes, or until the cookies are bumpy, rounded, and still a little soft to the touch. Cool on the baking sheets for 2 minutes, then transfer to wire racks to cool completely. Cool the baking sheets for 5 minutes before baking additional batches.

> **Recommended storage**
> *3 days at room temperature*
> *3 months in the freezer*

Personalize It!

To make fudgier Chocolate Coconut and Pecan Cookies, reduce the granulated sugar to ⅔ cup plus 1 tablespoon; beat in ⅓ cup packed dark brown sugar and 1 tablespoon light corn syrup with the granulated sugar.

To make crunchier Chocolate Coconut and Pecan Cookies, increase the unsalted butter to 8 tablespoons; use 2 large eggs plus 1 large egg white (rather than 3 whole eggs); and use unsweetened coconut flakes, rather than sweetened shredded coconut.

CHOCOLATE COCONUT COOKIES

These resemble Florida coconut patties, a candy with a rich, coconut center, surrounded by a thin chocolate shell. In our cookie version, a creamy coconut center, somewhat like coconut cheesecake, is surrounded by a moist chocolate cookie. We dare say they're just as irresistible.

MAKES ABOUT 2½ DOZEN LARGE COOKIES

FOR THE COCONUT FILLING

6	ounces cream cheese, softened
¾	cup sugar
1	large egg yolk, at room temperature
1½	teaspoons vanilla extract
2¼	cups unsweetened coconut chips (about 5 ounces, see page 19)

FOR THE CHOCOLATE COOKIES

1¾	cups all-purpose flour
⅓	cup cocoa powder, sifted
½	teaspoon baking soda
¼	teaspoon salt
12	tablespoons (1½ sticks) cool, unsalted butter, cut into small pieces
1	cup sugar
1	large egg, at room temperature

1. Position the rack in the center of the oven; preheat the oven to 375°F.

2. To make the coconut filling, beat the cream cheese and sugar in a large bowl, using an electric mixer at medium speed, until smooth and light, about 1 minute. Beat in the egg yolk, then the vanilla, until smooth. Finally, beat in the coconut chips at a very low speed just until evenly distributed. Set this mixture aside.

3. To make the chocolate cookies, whisk the flour, cocoa powder, baking soda, and salt in a medium bowl until uniform; set aside.

4. Clean and dry the beaters. Soften the butter in a second large bowl, using the electric mixer at medium speed, about 1 minute. Add the sugar and continue beating until light and airy but still a little grainy, about 1 more minute. Beat in the egg until smooth, no more than 20 seconds. Turn off the beaters, add the prepared flour mixture, and beat at a very low speed, just until well combined but not until not sticky. The dough should be stiff but still pliable.

5. Scoop out 1 tablespoon of the dough. Working in the palm of your hand or on a clean, dry work surface, flatten the dough into a circle about 2½ to 3 inches in diameter. Mound 2 teaspoons of the coconut filling in the middle of this circle, then fold the dough up onto the filling, making four sides that come up onto the filling but do not cover it, sort of like a little brown present (the chocolate dough) with tissue paper (the coconut filling) poofing out the top. Place the cookie on a large, ungreased baking sheet, preferably nonstick, then continue making the cookies, spacing them about 2 inches apart on the sheet.

6. Bake for 9 minutes, rotate the sheet back to front, and continue baking for about 9 more minutes, or until the cookies are set, just starting to brown along the edges, but still slightly springy to the touch. Cool on the baking sheet for 2 minutes, then transfer the cookies to a wire rack to cool completely. Cool the baking sheet for 5 minutes before making more filled cookies and baking them as directed, or use a second large baking sheet to make the second batch while the first bakes.

Recommended storage
3 days at room temperature
Not recommended for freezing

Mix It Up!
Chocolate Coconut Almond Cookies: Reduce the coconut to 1½ cups; add ½ cup ground almonds with the remaining coconut. Also add ½ teaspoon almond extract with the vanilla extract.

Chocolate Coconut Cookie Cups: Push a similar amount of dough into a mini muffin cup, rather than your hand; use your thumb to make a deep hole. Fill as directed with the coconut filling. Bake as directed and cool in the muffin tins before removing.

Chocolate Coconut Lime Cookies: Add 2 teaspoons grated lime zest and 1 teaspoon lime juice with the vanilla extract.

Chocolate Piña Colada Cookies: Reduce the coconut to 1½ cups; add ½ cup finely chopped dried pineapple with the remaining coconut. Substitute rum extract for the vanilla extract.

Double Chocolate Coconut Cookies: Stir 1 ounce unsweetened chocolate, melted and cooled, into the filling with the vanilla extract. Substitute sweetened coconut flakes for the unsweetened coconut chips.

CHOCOLATE COCONUT MACAROONS

There's a lot of cocoa powder in these macaroons. They have the deep, rich taste that is characteristic of macaroons found in German bakeshops. The cookies are flourless—so there's nothing to stand in the way of a good crunch. They don't freeze well, but we doubt you'll have any leftovers.

MAKES ABOUT 30 MACAROONS

- 4 large egg whites, at room temperature
- 1/8 teaspoon salt
- 1/2 teaspoon cream of tartar
- 1 cup sugar
- One 14-ounce package sweetened shredded coconut
- 3/4 cup plus 2 tablespoons cocoa powder, sifted

1. Position the rack in the center of the oven. Preheat the oven to 350°F. Line a large baking sheet with parchment paper or a silicone baking mat; set aside.

2. Beat the egg whites and salt in a large bowl with an electric mixer at low speed until frothy. Add the cream of tartar, increase the speed to high, and beat until soft peaks form, about 2 minutes. Scrape down the sides of the bowl, then add the sugar in 1-tablespoon increments, beating all the while. Continue beating until the sugar has completely dissolved, about 3 to 5 more minutes—you can tell by rubbing a small amount of the mixture between your fingers to feel any grains.

3. Gently fold in the coconut with a rubber spatula, then the cocoa powder, taking care not to deflate the egg whites, working in long, sweeping arcs without pressing into the batter; however, make sure the cocoa powder is incorporated into the batter, although a few white streaks may still be visible.

4. Drop by rounded but spiky tablespoonfuls onto the prepared baking sheet, spacing the mounds about 1 inch apart. Bake for 10 minutes. Rotate the sheet top to bottom and back to front, then continue baking about another 10 minutes, or until dry and firm. Cool on the baking sheet for about 10 minutes, or until they are easy to remove. Cool the cookies completely on wire racks. Cool the baking sheets completely before baking additional batches, if necessary.

Recommended storage
3 days at room temperature
Not recommended for freezing

Chocolate-Dipped Macaroons!

You can dip these macaroons in melted chocolate for an even more decadent treat. Melt 12 ounces semisweet, bittersweet, or white chocolate in a double boiler set over a small amount of simmering water; stir until half the chocolate is melted, then continue stirring off the heat until it is fully melted. Cool for 5 minutes. Dip the cookies into the melted chocolate by holding them at the tops and dipping the bottoms into the chocolate, until the cookies are coated halfway up the sides. Shake off any excess chocolate, then set them on wax paper to firm, about 1 hour.

CHOCOLATE CORNMEAL COOKIES

hese cookies are unusual but delicious all the same. The cornmeal makes them very crunchy—not like the snap of butter cookies, but stronger and heartier. The assertive flavor of cornmeal is balanced by orange zest and orange flower water. The dough sets up stiff—you'll need to bake it all once you've chilled it in the refrigerator for 30 minutes.

MAKES ABOUT 4 DOZEN COOKIES

2¼	cups all-purpose flour
1	cup yellow cornmeal
¾	cup cornstarch
¼	teaspoon salt
3	ounces unsweetened chocolate, chopped
½	pound (2 sticks) cool, unsalted butter, cut into small pieces
1¼	cups sugar
2	large eggs, at room temperature
1	large egg yolk, at room temperature
2	tablespoons finely grated orange zest
1	teaspoon orange flower water or ½ teaspoon orange extract

1. Position the rack in the center of the oven and preheat the oven to 350°F. Whisk the flour, cornmeal, cornstarch, and salt in a medium bowl; set aside.

2. Place the chocolate in the top half of a double boiler set over about 2 inches of simmering water, or in a medium bowl that fits tightly over a medium saucepan with a similar amount of simmering water. Stir until half the chocolate has melted, then remove the double boiler's top half or the bowl from the heat—be careful of any escaping steam, which can condense and cause the chocolate to seize—and continue stirring until all the chocolate has melted. Set aside to cool for 5 minutes, stirring occasionally.

3. Soften the butter in a large bowl, using an electric mixer at medium speed, about 1 minute. Add the sugar and continue beating just until fluffy, about 1 minute. Beat in the eggs one at a time, then the egg yolk; continue beating until it looks fairly smooth. Beat in the melted chocolate by pouring it into the bowl in a thin, steady stream while the beaters are running at low speed; scrape down the sides of the bowl as necessary. Beat in the orange zest and orange flower water or orange extract until smooth. Turn off the beaters, add the flour, and beat at low speed until a soft, workable dough forms. Gather into a ball in the bowl, then cover the bowl loosely with a clean kitchen towel and refrigerate just until firm, about 30 minutes.

4. Roll 2 teaspoons of the dough into a ball, then place on a large ungreased baking sheet, preferably nonstick. Continue making balls, spacing them 1½ inches apart on the baking sheet. Press the balls with a fork, creating a cross-hatch pattern by pressing down one direction, then rotating the tines 90 degrees and pressing again. Press gently, just until the dough flattens somewhat and cracks a little at the edges.

5. Bake for 11 minutes, rotating the sheet back to front halfway through baking, until the cookies are dry and somewhat firm to the touch. Cool on the baking sheet for 2 minutes, then transfer to a wire rack to cool completely. Cool the baking sheet for 5 minutes before baking additional batches on it, or work with a second large baking sheet, making a second batch while the first bakes.

Recommended storage
4 days at room temperature
3 months in the freezer

Farther Afield!
For an exotic treat, omit the orange zest and orange flower water; beat in 2 teaspoons rose water in their place.

For a Provençal flavor, add 1 tablespoon finely chopped rosemary with the orange zest.

CHOCOLATE CREAM CHEESE REFRIGERATOR COOKIES

These simple cookies are all about instant gratification—especially if you've made the dough in advance! You can keep it in your refrigerator for up to 5 days, slicing off as much you need to bake as many cookies as you want. In other words, cookies at your whim.

MAKES ABOUT 6 DOZEN COOKIES

2½	ounces unsweetened chocolate, chopped
8	tablespoons (1 stick) cool, unsalted butter, cut into small pieces
4	tablespoons solid vegetable shortening (2 ounces)
3	ounces cream cheese (regular or low-fat, but not nonfat), softened
¾	cup plus 1 tablespoon granulated sugar
¼	cup packed dark brown sugar
1	large egg, at room temperature
1	teaspoon vanilla extract
½	teaspoon salt
2¾	cups all-purpose flour

1. Place the chopped chocolate in the top half of a double boiler set over about 1 inch of simmering water, or in a medium bowl that fits tightly over a medium pot with about the same amount of simmering water. Stir until half the chocolate has melted, then remove the double boiler's top half or the bowl from the heat and continue stirring until all the chocolate has melted. Set aside to cool for 5 minutes.

2. Beat the butter, shortening, and cream cheese in a large bowl with an electric mixer at medium speed until smooth, about 1 minute. Beat in both sugars; continue beating until airy and pale brown, about 1 more minute. Beat in the egg, vanilla, and salt; then slowly pour in the melted chocolate, beating until it looks smooth. Finally, turn off the beaters, add the flour, and beat at very low speed just until a soft but workable dough forms. Divide this dough in half; shape each half into a log about 9 inches long and 2 inches in diameter. Wrap each in plastic wrap and refrigerate at least 3 hours or up to 5 days.

3. Position the rack in the center of the oven; preheat the oven to 375°F.

4. Unwrap one of the logs and slice off ¼-inch-thick cookie disks. Place them on a large ungreased baking sheet, preferably nonstick, spacing them about 1½ inches apart. Rewrap the remaining dough and return it to the refrigerator.

5. Bake for 10 minutes, reversing the sheet back to front once halfway through baking. When done, the cookies should be soft and slightly springy to the touch. Cool on the baking sheet for 2 minutes, then transfer to a wire rack to cool completely. Cool the baking sheet for 5 minutes before baking additional batches, if desired.

Recommended storage
3 days at room temperature
Once baked, 2 months in the freezer

More Choices!
Chocolate Chip Cream Cheese Refrigerator Cookies: Mix 1 cup mini chocolate chips with the flour.

Chocolate Cream Cheese Refrigerator Sandwich Cookies: Make the chocolate filling for Chocolate Cream Sandwich Cookies (page 77). Each sandwich should have 2 teaspoons of this filling between two of these refrigerator cookies.

Chocolate Hanukkah Gelt: Brush the baked, cooled cookies with edible gold dust, or paint them with edible gold paint. Or, to be very fancy, lay a small sheet of edible gold leaf over each cookie.

Chocolate Mint Cream Cheese Refrigerator Cookies: Substitute ½ teaspoon mint extract for the vanilla extract.

CHOCOLATE CREAM
SANDWICH COOKIES

These are classic: a dense, dark cookie with a creamy sandwich center. To get the taste and texture of a commercial cream sandwich cookie, we've left out any egg or leavening, so the cookies themselves are flat and crunchy, a great foil to the filling.

MAKES ABOUT 20 LARGE SANDWICH COOKIES

FOR THE COOKIES

1½	cups all-purpose flour
¾	cup cocoa powder, preferably Dutch-processed, sifted
½	teaspoon salt
1	cup solid vegetable shortening (8 ounces)
1	cup plus 2 tablespoons confectioners' sugar
1	teaspoon vanilla extract

FOR THE FILLING

4½	tablespoons solid vegetable shortening (slightly more than 2 ounces)
1	tablespoon light corn syrup
1½	cups confectioners' sugar, or more if necessary
1	tablespoon vanilla extract
⅛	teaspoon salt

1. Whisk the flour, cocoa powder, and salt in a medium bowl until uniform; set aside.

2. Use an electric mixer at medium speed to beat the shortening and confectioners' sugar in a large bowl until light and very fluffy, about 2 minutes. Scrape down the sides of the bowl and beat in the vanilla until smooth. Remove the beaters and stir in the prepared flour mixture with a wooden spoon or rubber spatula just until incorporated. The dough will be quite soft, but it will hold together into a ball. Divide in half.

3. Sprinkle a few drops of water on your work surface, then cover with a large sheet of plastic wrap. Place half the dough on it, then lay a second large sheet of plastic wrap on top. Roll out the dough until ¼ inch thick. Transfer the dough, still between the sheets of plastic wrap, to a large baking sheet; place in the refrigerator for 1 hour, or until firm. Repeat this step with the second half of the dough, transferring it, sandwiched between sheets of plastic wrap, to a second baking sheet also placed in the refrigerator.

4. Position the rack in the center of the oven; preheat the oven to 350°F.

5. Remove the rolled-out dough from the refrigerator, peel off the top sheet of plastic wrap, and use a 2½-inch, round cookie cutter to cut out cookies. Use a metal spatula to transfer them to a large, ungreased baking sheet, preferably nonstick, spacing them about 2 inches apart. Work quickly here—you want the cookies to be cool when they go into the oven. Also, use the same baking sheet that held the dough in the refrigerator—it will be cool and prevent the cookies from spreading while baking. Prick each disk with a fork, thereby creating a decorative cross-hatch pattern on the cookie. If there are dough scraps, you can reroll them, but you need to roll them out again between pieces of plastic wrap, then refrigerate for about 1 hour, or until firm.

6. Bake for 12 minutes, rotating the sheet back to front halfway through baking. The cookies will be firm but a little spongy—they will crisp as they cool. Cool for 3 minutes on the baking sheet, then transfer to a wire rack to cool completely. Place the baking sheet in the refrigerator and chill it for 5 minutes before baking additional batches—or use the second baking sheet, with the second sheet of dough that's already in the refrigerator.

7. Once all the cookies are baked and cooled, prepare the filling by beating the shortening and corn syrup in a medium bowl until smooth, using an electric mixer at medium speed. Beat in the confectioners' sugar until fluffy, then beat in the vanilla and salt until smooth. You may need to add a little more confectioners' sugar to get a spreadable, frosting-like consistency—but be careful of adding too much, as it will continue to harden as it sets.

8. To fill, place a heaping teaspoonful of the filling mixture on the flat side of one of the cookies. Spread this gently to the ends, using a small flatware knife or an off-set spatula, making an even layer of filling. Top with a second cookie, flat side down; place on a wire rack to let the filling set somewhat, about 15 minutes. Continue creating chocolate cream sandwiches until all the cookies and filling are used.

> **Recommended storage**
> *2 days at room temperature*
> *If filled, 1 month in the freezer; the cookies alone can be frozen for up to 3 months, then thawed and sandwiched with filling as directed*

Customize It!

Because the cookies here are classics, we recommend varying only the cream filling. To do so, omit the vanilla extract from the filling and in its place, add one of the following: ½ teaspoon banana flavoring, ½ teaspoon almond extract, 1 teaspoon maple extract, 1 teaspoon rum extract, ½ teaspoon lemon extract with 1 drop yellow food coloring, ½ teaspoon mint extract with 1 drop green food coloring, ½ teaspoon orange extract with 1 drop orange food coloring, or ½ teaspoon cherry flavoring with 1 drop red food coloring.

CHOCOLATE CRINKLES

These round disks have a delicate crisp crunch, yet remain intensely soft and moist inside. Sifting the dry ingredients is important because you want the flour to be finely aerated. The batter needs to be refrigerated a few hours before baking, so give yourself leeway by making it ahead.

MAKES ABOUT 6 DOZEN COOKIES

2	cups all-purpose flour
2	cups confectioners' sugar
½	cup cocoa powder, preferably Dutch-processed, sifted
2	teaspoons baking powder
½	teaspoon salt
4	ounces unsweetened chocolate, chopped
4	tablespoons (½ stick) unsalted butter, cut into small pieces
1½	cups packed light brown sugar
⅓	cup light corn syrup
2	teaspoons vanilla extract
4	large egg whites, at room temperature

1. Spread a sheet of wax paper on your work surface. Sift the flour, 1½ cups of the confectioners' sugar, the cocoa powder, baking powder, and salt together, using a flour sifter or a fine-mesh sieve, allowing the sifted mixture to fall onto the wax paper. Repeat, making sure the cocoa powder is evenly distributed through the mixture. Set aside.

2. Place the chocolate and butter in the top of a double boiler or in a medium bowl that fits securely over a medium saucepan. Bring about 1-inch of water to a boil in the bottom of the double boiler or in the saucepan; place the top of the double boiler or the bowl over the simmering water, reduce the heat but maintain the boil, and stir until half the chocolate has melted. Remove the top of the double boiler or the bowl from over the water—be careful of any escaping steam—and continue stirring off the heat until all the chocolate and butter have melted and the mixture is smooth. Transfer to the bowl of a standing mixer, or to a large, clean bowl if you're using a handheld mixer, and cool for 5 minutes.

3. Beat the brown sugar into the chocolate mixture, using an electric mixer at medium speed, until light and silky, about 1 minute. Beat in the corn syrup and vanilla. Scrape down the sides of the bowl, then beat in the egg whites all at once until smooth, a little less than 1 minute.

4. Remove the beaters and stir in the prepared flour mixture, using a wooden spoon or stiff spatula; stir just until any trace of flour has disappeared. Cover the bowl with a clean kitchen towel and set in the refrigerator until the mixture becomes firm, at least 1 hour but no more than 8 hours.

5. Arrange an oven rack in the center of the oven; preheat the oven to 350°F. Line a baking sheet with parchment paper or a silicone baking mat; set aside. Place the remaining ½ cup confectioners' sugar in a small bowl; set aside as well.

6. Roll a small piece of the firm dough into a small ball, about the size of a large olive. Roll this ball in the confectioners' sugar, then place it on the prepared baking sheet. Continue making sugared balls, spacing them about 1½ inches apart, until the baking sheet is full. (It may be easier to make all the balls first, then roll them in the confectioners' sugar—you are less likely to transfer confectioners' sugar back into the chocolate dough.) Return any unused dough to the refrigerator.

7. Bake for about 16 minutes, or until the cookies have spread and cracked at the edges and are somewhat firm to the touch. Cool for 5 minutes on the baking sheet, then carefully transfer them to a wire rack using a metal spatula (they are still a little fragile because they're so fudgy). Let the baking sheet cool for 5 minutes before baking additional batches; if using parchment paper, replace it with a new sheet. Let the baked cookies cool completely on the wire rack.

Recommended storage
5 days at room temperature
Not recommended for freezing

CHOCOLATE FORTUNE COOKIES

You have to move fast to get the fortunes inside these crunchy wonders, so write them out before you make the cookies. You can only bake one cookie at a time because you need to work without delay to fold the cookie up when it comes out of the oven.

MAKES 1 DOZEN LARGE COOKIES

Unsalted butter, for greasing the baking sheets or nonstick spray
2   large egg whites, at room temperature
2   teaspoons chocolate extract (see Note), or vanilla extract
⅛   teaspoon salt
¼   cup plus 2 tablespoons all-purpose flour
2   tablespoons cocoa powder, sifted
½   cup superfine sugar (see page 21)
12   prepared fortunes (see page 83)

1. Position the rack in the center of the oven; preheat the oven to 375°F. Butter two baking sheets, preferably nonstick; set aside.

2. Use a fork to beat the egg whites, chocolate or vanilla extract, and salt in a medium bowl until frothy. Place the flour, cocoa powder, and sugar in a fine-mesh sieve and sift it into the egg-white mixture. Stir with a wooden spoon until smooth.

3. Place 1 heaping teaspoon of batter on one of the prepared baking sheets, then use an offset spatula to smooth the batter into a 5-inch-diameter, paper-thin circle. Bake for 5 minutes until set and somewhat dry. Meanwhile, repeat the process on the other cookie sheet to create a second circle.

4. When the cookie comes out the oven, let it cool on the sheet for just 5 to 10 seconds, or until you can handle it. Meanwhile, start baking the second cookie.

5. Lay the fortune in the center of the baked cookie, then use a thin metal spatula to loosen the cookie from the sheet. Fold one-half of the cookie up and over, to create a half-moon, but leaving a finger-width pocket at the bottom of the circle where the fortune is now enclosed. Then fold each "wing" of the half-moon up toward the center, so that they meet above the cookie, thereby making a rather large fortune cookie. Transfer to a wire rack to cool completely. Cool the baking sheet for 5 minutes before cleaning it, drying it thoroughly, and buttering it again. Keep working in this pattern—one cookie baking, one baked cookie being formed—until all the batter is used. Cool the cookies completely on the wire rack before storing.

NOTE: *Chocolate extract is a professional baker's secret—a distillate from roasted cocoa beans. It's found in almost all baking supply stores and some gourmet markets.*

Recommended storage
2 days at room temperature
Not recommended for freezing

Fortunes
Cut a small piece of paper into strips about 5 inches × ½ inch. If using colored paper, make sure it is made with food-safe dyes. Write or type the "fortune" on the thin strip. Fortunes might include:

Absence makes the heart go awander.

All's fair in love and shopping.

Do you want a boy or a girl?

I got a sitter so we can go out dancing.

I'll let you guess what's the only thing better than cookies.

Meet me in the bedroom.

Some things are meant to be—like us.

Thank God you're not the man I married.

We're so happy you're in our lives.

Will you marry me?

You should see the kitchen after making these cookies.

CHOCOLATE GINGERBREAD MEN

Here's a classic cookie that's even better when made with chocolate. The extra dryness in cocoa powder means you don't have to refrigerate the dough to firm it up before you roll it out. You could decorate with the standard candy accoutrements, or use your imagination (we've also included a simple frosting recipe). And don't feel bound by the gingerbread man shape—you could easily make any other shape, provided you use a large cookie cutter.

MAKES ABOUT 24 LARGE GINGERBREAD MEN

3¼ cups plus 2 tablespoons all-purpose flour, plus additional for dusting

⅔ cup cocoa powder, preferably natural cocoa powder, sifted

1 tablespoon ground ginger (see Note)

1 teaspoon ground cinnamon

1 teaspoon baking soda

1 teaspoon salt

½ teaspoon baking powder

½ teaspoon ground cloves

⅔ cup solid vegetable shortening (5⅓ ounces), plus additional for greasing the baking sheet

½ cup packed dark brown sugar

1 large egg, at room temperature

¾ cup unsulphured molasses

Raisins and red hot candies for garnish

1. Position the racks in the top and bottom thirds of the oven; preheat the oven to 375°F. Use a dab of shortening on a small sheet of wax paper to grease a large baking sheet; set aside. Whisk the flour, cocoa powder, ground ginger, cinnamon, baking soda, salt, baking powder, and cloves in a large bowl until the spices and cocoa are evenly distributed; set aside as well.

2. Cream the shortening and brown sugar in a second large bowl, using an electric mixer at medium speed, until smooth and airy, about 1 minute. Beat in the egg, then the molasses. Turn off the mixer, add the prepared flour mixture, and then beat at very low speed just until crumbly bits of dough form, but not until the mass begins to cohere into a ball.

3. Lightly dust a clean, dry work surface and your hands with flour. Turn the dough out and knead just until it forms a smooth mass, about 30 seconds. Divide in thirds and cover them with a clean kitchen towel.

4. Lightly dust the work surface again with flour and roll one of the thirds to a rectangle about ¼ inch thick. Flour the dough and the rolling pin only as necessary. Use a large gingerbread-man cookie cutter to cut the dough into the desired shapes, then use a metal spatula to transfer them carefully to the prepared baking sheet. Gather any scraps, lightly dust again with flour, and roll out a second time, creating additional gingerbread men. Decorate the cookies with the raisins and red hots. For gingerbread men, make raisin eyes and red hot mouths; or raisin eyes and mouths, then use the red hots for buttons on their coats.

5. Bake for 4 minutes, then rotate the sheets top to bottom and front to back. Bake for another 4 minutes, or until the cookies feel dry but still a little soft. Cool on the baking sheets for 2 minutes, then transfer to wire racks to cool completely. Cool the baking sheets for 5 more minutes and regrease them before baking additional batches, as necessary; or work with two baking sheets, preparing one while the other bakes.

NOTE: *Because of the interaction of essential oils, ground ginger goes stale quickly. For the best flavor, make sure yours is fresh—no more than 2 months from purchase.*

Recommended storage
2 days at room temperature
1 month in the freezer

A Simple Chocolate Frosting

MAKES ABOUT ¾ CUP

You can bake the gingerbread men without any decoration, and then frost them before sticking on the red hots and other candies—just make sure the cookies are completely cool before frosting them. We suggest this simple recipe, guaranteed to up the chocolate quotient quite a bit and satisfy all the little chocoholics in your life. The frosting hardens fast, so use it the moment it's ready.

2 tablespoons unsalted butter, at room temperature
3 tablespoons cocoa powder, sifted
1½ tablespoons heavy cream
1½ teaspoons light corn syrup
1 teaspoon vanilla extract
¾ cup confectioners' sugar

1. In a large bowl, beat the butter, cocoa powder, cream, corn syrup, and vanilla with an electric mixer at medium speed; continue beating until smooth and thick, about 4 minutes, scraping down the sides of the bowl as necessary.

2. Beat in the sugar, ½ cup at a time, allowing each addition to be fully incorporated before adding the next. Beat an additional minute once all the sugar is incorporated; spread immediately on the cooled cookies using an offset or icing spatula.

CHOCOLATE GINGERSNAPS

Here's the classic gingersnap with a chocolate twist. The cookies are thin, waferlike, and crisp, spiked with molasses and ginger. With a cup of tea, they're the perfect antidote to a cold winter night—or the right accompaniment to a crisp fall afternoon.

MAKES ABOUT 3 DOZEN SMALL COOKIES

Nonstick spray

1¼	cups all-purpose flour, plus additional for dusting
3	tablespoons cocoa powder, preferably natural, sifted
2	teaspoons ground ginger (see Note, page 85)
½	teaspoon grated nutmeg
¼	teaspoon baking powder
¼	teaspoon salt
¼	cup solid vegetable shortening (2 ounces)
¼	cup molasses, preferably unsulphured
¼	cup packed dark brown sugar
1	large egg white, at room temperature

1. Position the racks in the bottom and top thirds of the oven. Preheat the oven to 350°F. Spray two large baking sheets with nonstick spray; set aside. Mix the flour, cocoa powder, ginger, nutmeg, baking powder, and salt in a medium bowl until uniform; set aside as well.

2. Beat the shortening, molasses, and brown sugar in a large bowl until creamy, using an electric mixer at medium speed. Continue beating until amber brown and very fluffy, about 2 minutes. Beat in the egg white.

3. Remove the beaters and stir in the prepared flour mixture with a wooden spoon or a rubber spatula. Stir just until thick and lush if still slightly grainy—the batter should be the same color it was before the flour was added; it should not lighten.

4. Dust a clean, dry work surface with flour, then gather the dough into a ball, place it on the work surface, and press down lightly with your hands, just until it looks like a flattened basketball. Dust a rolling pin lightly with flour, dust the top of the dough itself with a fine film of flour, then roll it out to a large circle, about 16 inches in diameter and ¼ inch thick (see Note).

5. Using a 2-inch cookie cutter or a glass with a 2-inch-diameter lip, cut out round cookie disks, then transfer them to the prepared baking sheets, spacing them about 1 inch apart. If desired, reroll the dough scraps, dusting lightly with flour, to create more cookies.

6. Bake for 4 minutes, then rotate the sheets top to bottom and back to front. Continue baking for about 4 more minutes, or until the cookies are firm and crisp. Cool on the baking sheets for 1 minute, then gently transfer the cookies to wire racks to cool. If baking additional batches, allow the baking sheets to cool to room temperature, then spray them with nonstick spray again before proceeding.

NOTE: *For crackerlike cookies, roll the dough even thinner, to about ⅛-inch thickness. Reduce the baking time by 1 minute.*

Recommended storage
1 week at room temperature
3 months in the freezer

Customize It!

Make sandwich cookies using the white cream filling from the Chocolate Cream Sandwich Cookies (page 77). Add 1 teaspoon ground ginger to the filling with the confectioners' sugar.

Ice the cookies with the white icing in the Black Black and Whites (page 33). Omit the chocolate from the icing and simply make a large batch of the white vanilla icing. Let the iced cookies stand on a wire rack, set over a sheet of wax paper, for about 1 hour, or until the icing has hardened.

CHOCOLATE GINGER SUGAR COOKIES

These cookies look like traditional snickerdoodles, cracked and cakey on the outside, but they're far softer and more luscious inside, like a sugar cookie enhanced with ginger. They're best warm, right out of the oven, but you can store them for days if you want to space out your indulgences.

MAKES ABOUT 4 DOZEN COOKIES

1¾	cups all-purpose flour
½	cup cocoa powder, sifted
½	teaspoon baking soda
½	teaspoon salt
1½	cups sugar
1	tablespoon plus 2 teaspoons ground ginger (see Note, page 85)
8	tablespoons (1 stick) cool, unsalted butter, cut into small pieces, plus additional for buttering the baking sheets
2	large eggs, at room temperature
1	tablespoon vanilla extract

1. Position the racks in the top and bottom thirds of the oven. Preheat the oven to 350°F. Lightly butter two large baking sheets; set them aside. Whisk the flour, cocoa powder, baking soda, and salt in a medium bowl until evenly colored; set aside. Finally, mix ¼ cup of the sugar with 2 teaspoons ginger in a small bowl or a soup dish; set aside.

2. Soften the butter in a large bowl, using an electric mixer at medium speed. Add the remaining 1¼ cups sugar and beat until fluffy and pale yellow, about 1 minute. Beat in the eggs one at a time, making sure the first is fully incorporated before adding the second; then beat in the vanilla. Turn off the mixer, add the prepared flour mixture, and beat in at a very low speed just until a fudgy, not sticky, dough forms, about the consistency of soft marzipan.

3. Roll heaping teaspoonfuls of the dough into balls, then roll them in the sugar/ginger mixture, giving them a fine, light coating. It's easier to make all the balls you need first, clean and dry your hands, and then roll the balls in the sugar mixture—that way, you're not going back and forth and getting the sugar all over your dough-covered hands. Place the balls on the prepared sheets, spacing them about 1½ inches apart.

4. Bake for 6 minutes, then rotate the sheets top to bottom and back to front. Continue baking for about 6 more minutes, or until the tops are cracked, but the cookies themselves are still slightly soft to the touch, permitting small indentions. Cool on the baking sheets for 5 minutes, then transfer to a wire rack to cool. The baking sheets should be cooled completely before you bake additional batches, lightly buttering them before using them again.

Recommended storage
4 days at room temperature
3 months in the freezer

Customize It!
Mix ½ cup of any of the following into the batter with the prepared flour mixture: chopped dried apricots, chopped dried figs, chopped dried pears, chopped pitted dates, dried blueberries, dried cranberries, or dried currants.

CHOCOLATE GRAHAM CRACKER COOKIES

These simple chocolate disks have the distinctive taste and crunch of graham crackers. They are perfect with a glass of cold milk.

MAKES ABOUT 3 DOZEN COOKIES

2	cups plus 2 tablespoons all-purpose flour
1½	cups graham cracker crumbs (see Note)
⅓	cup cocoa powder, preferably natural, sifted
½	teaspoon salt
½	pound (2 sticks) cool, unsalted butter, cut into small pieces
1½	cups granulated sugar
¼	cup packed light brown sugar
2	large egg yolks, at room temperature
1	teaspoon vanilla extract

1. Position the racks in the top and bottom thirds of the oven; preheat the oven to 350°F. Whisk the flour, graham cracker crumbs, cocoa powder, and salt in a large bowl until well combined; set aside.

2. Soften the butter in a large bowl, using an electric mixer at medium speed, until smooth and light, about 1 minute. Add both sugars and continue beating at medium speed until fluffy, if a little grainy, about 1 more minute. Add the egg yolks and vanilla; beat until smooth. Add the flour mixture and beat at low speed until the dough forms into crumbs. Remove the beaters and work the dough with your hands in the bowl until it comes together into a ball. The dough will be dry and stiff. Divide it into thirds and cover loosely with a clean kitchen towel.

3. Sprinkle a few drops of water on your work surface, then lay a large sheet of wax paper across it (the water will help the wax paper stay in place as you roll the dough). Place one of the pieces of dough on top of the wax paper, flatten the dough slightly, and cover with a second sheet of wax paper. Roll into a circle about 11 inches in diameter and ¼ inch thick. Remove the top sheet of wax paper and use a drinking glass or round cookie cutter to cut the dough into 3-inch circles—or use the cookie cutter of your choice (heart, Christmas tree, or whale, for example) that yields about the same size cookies. Use a metal spatula to transfer the cookies to two large, ungreased baking sheets, preferably nonstick, spacing the cookies about 1½ inches apart. Repeat this process with additional pieces of dough until you have filled both sheets; set the remainder of the dough aside for a second baking.

4. Bake for 6 minutes, then rotate the sheets top to bottom and back to front. Continue baking for about 6 more minutes, or until set but still springy to the touch. Do not overbake. Cool the cookies on the baking sheets for 3 minutes, then transfer to wire racks to cool completely. Cool the baking sheets before using them again. Repeat the rolling-out and baking process, using the remainder of the dough.

NOTE: *You can use purchased graham cracker crumbs, or you can pulse 12 whole graham crackers in a food processor fitted with the chopping blade for about the right amount of crumbs. Do not use low-fat graham crackers for this recipe.*

Recommended storage
5 days at room temperature
3 months in the freezer

Personalize It!
Make sandwich cookies using 2 teaspoons of almond butter, Marshmallow Fluff, Nutella, orange marmalade, peanut butter, or raspberry jam for each sandwich cookie (you'll need about ¾ cup total volume).

CHOCOLATE HAZELNUT BISCOTTI

These traditional, twice-baked Italian cookies are packed with hazelnuts, which soften considerably during baking, allowing you to slice the cookies cleanly, provided you have a sharp, serrated knife on hand. Don't forget to dunk!

MAKES ABOUT 2 DOZEN LARGE BISCOTTI

3	cups all-purpose flour, plus additional for dusting
1⅔	cups sugar
1	cup cocoa powder, preferably Dutch-processed, sifted
2	teaspoons baking powder
½	teaspoon salt
2	cups whole hazelnuts (about 10 ounces)
4	large eggs, at room temperature
6	tablespoons hazelnut oil (see Note) or canola oil
1	tablespoon vanilla extract

1. Position the rack in the center of the oven. Preheat the oven to 350°F. Whisk the flour, sugar, cocoa powder, baking powder, and salt in a large bowl until a uniform color; set aside.

2. Place the hazelnuts on a large baking sheet and toast for about 7 minutes, or until very aromatic and lightly browned. Do not allow the pale creamy flesh of the nuts to turn dark brown. Cool them, then pour them into a clean kitchen towel and rub off the papery skins, working in batches if necessary. (One word of warning: keep your lips sealed because bits of that papery stuff can make for a coughing nightmare!) You needn't get every single bit of husk off, but do a fairly thorough job. Set the cleaned, toasted nuts aside. Once the baking sheet has cooled, line it with parchment paper or a silicone baking mat.

3. With an electric mixer at medium speed, beat the eggs and oil in a second large bowl until yellow and light, about 2 minutes. Scrape down the sides of the bowl, then beat in the vanilla until smooth. Turn off the beaters, add the flour mixture all at once, then beat at low speed just until small, wet bits of dough start to cohere, about 15 seconds. Remove the beaters and stir in the hazelnuts with a wooden spoon, or work them in by hand.

4. Lightly dust a clean, dry work surface with flour, then turn the dough out onto it. Handling it as little as possible, gather the dough into a ball, making sure the nuts are evenly distributed. Do not knead the dough. Dust the work surface and your hands again with flour, then divide the dough in half and form each into a 10-inch log. Flatten the logs slightly, so that they become oval cylinders, about 1 inch thick at their centers.

5. Place these logs on the prepared baking sheet and bake for about 35 minutes, or until cracked and firm to the touch, but not browned. Cool on the sheet for 20 minutes until barely warm. Meanwhile, lower the oven temperature to 300°F.

6. Transfer the logs to a cutting board and slice them with a serrated knife into ¾-inch-thick cookies. If desired, slice them on the diagonal for longer biscotti. Place the cookies, cut side down and about ½ inch apart, on the baking sheet, still covered with parchment or a baking mat. If one baking sheet is not large enough to hold all the biscotti, do a second baking after the first has finished.

7. Bake for 8 minutes, then turn the cookies over to the other cut side, and bake for about 8 more minutes, or until toasted brown. Cool for 5 minutes on the sheet, then transfer to a wire rack and cool completely.

NOTE: *Hazelnut oil is found in most gourmet markets and some health food stores. It goes rancid quickly, so store it in the refrigerator, but let it come to room temperature before using. Always smell nut oils before you use them to make sure they don't have a sharp tang, a sign they've gone bad.*

More Fun!

To make dipped biscotti, place 12 ounces bittersweet, semisweet, milk, or white chocolate in the top half of a double boiler set over simmering water, or a medium bowl set over a saucepan with a small amount of simmering water; stir until half the chocolate has melted, then remove from the heat and continue stirring until all the chocolate has melted. Cool for 5 minutes. Dip the cooled biscotti into the chocolate, then place the cookies on large sheets of wax paper for about 30 minutes until the chocolate coating hardens.

CHOCOLATE HAZELNUT
SANDWICH COOKIES

These special treats are made with two very short (that is, crisp and a little grainy) hazelnut chocolate cookies sandwiching a mixture of Nutella and chocolate. But if you're in the mood for something simpler, just make the cookies on their own. They're nutty and light—perfect for spreading with plain Nutella or strawberry jam.

MAKES ABOUT 2 DOZEN SANDWICH COOKIES

FOR THE COOKIES

- 2 cups plus 2 tablespoons all-purpose flour, plus additional for dusting
- 2½ ounces semisweet chocolate, grated (see Chocolate Grater, page 15)
- ¼ teaspoon salt
- ½ cup whole hazelnuts
- 8 tablespoons (1 stick) cool, unsalted butter, cut into small pieces
- ½ cup solid vegetable shortening (4 ounces)
- ⅓ cup plus 1 tablespoon sugar
- 1 teaspoon vanilla extract

FOR THE FILLING

- 3 ounces bittersweet or semisweet chocolate, chopped
- ½ cup plus 2 tablespoons Nutella, or other hazelnut-chocolate spread

1. Position the racks in the top and bottom thirds of the oven. Preheat the oven to 350°F. Whisk the flour, grated chocolate, and salt in a medium bowl until uniform. Set aside, preferably out of the kitchen heat.

2. Place the hazelnuts on a large, lipped baking sheet, then toast them in the top third of the oven for about 10 minutes, or until lightly browned and fragrant, stirring occasionally. Cool the nuts on the baking sheet for about 5 minutes, then pour them into a clean kitchen towel. Gather the towel up and rub gently, thereby removing the hazelnuts' papery hulls. Place the hulled hazelnuts in a food processor fitted with a chopping blade and pulse on and off until the nuts are finely ground. Set aside.

3. Soften the butter and shortening by placing them in a large bowl and beating with an electric mixer at medium speed until light and creamy, about 1 minute. Add the sugar and continue beating until fluffy, about 1 minute. Mix in the ground hazelnuts, then the vanilla. Turn off the beaters, add the flour mixture, and beat at very low speed just until a dry dough forms.

4. Lightly dust a clean, dry work surface with flour, then turn the dough out onto it. Knead two or three times. Don't press down—you want the dough to come together, but you don't want the chocolate to melt. Divide the dough in half.

5. Place a large sheet of plastic wrap on your work surface, place one of the halves of dough at its center, then cover with a second large sheet of plastic wrap. Use a rolling pin to roll the dough out into a circle about 12 inches in diameter and ¼ inch thick. Peel off the top sheet of plastic wrap, then cut the dough into 2½-inch circles, using a cookie cutter or the lip of a similarly sized drinking glass. Use a metal spatula to transfer these circles to two large, ungreased cookie sheets, preferably nonstick, spacing the disks about 1 inch apart. The disks are fragile, so handle them as little as possible. Repeat this rolling and cutting process with the other half of the dough, either on two more baking sheets while the first cookies bake or filling out the first two baking sheets with more disks, space permitting. You can also reroll any dough scraps, if desired.

6. Bake for 6 minutes, then reverse the sheets back to front and top to bottom. Continue baking for about 5 minutes, or until the cookies are lightly browned and firm to the touch. Cool for 1 minute on the baking sheets, then transfer the cookies to a wire rack to cool completely. Cool the sheets for 5 minutes before baking additional batches.

7. When the cookies are cooled, make the filling by placing the chocolate in the top half of a double boiler set over about 1 inch of simmering water, or in a medium bowl that fits securely over a medium saucepan with about the same amount of simmering water. Stir until half the chocolate has melted, then remove the double boiler's top half or the bowl from the heat and continue stirring until all the chocolate has melted. Cool for 5 minutes, then stir in the Nutella or other hazelnut/chocolate spread until smooth.

8. Spread the flat side of one of the cookies with about 1 rounded teaspoon of the chocolate filling, taking care to even out the filling with an offset or rubber spatula. Top with a second cookie, flat side down. Set on a wire rack until the filling sets, about 15 minutes provided the room is cool. Repeat, making the remainder of the sandwich cookies.

Recommended storage
3 days at room temperature
Not recommended for freezing when filled; the plain wafers can be stored for up to 3 months in the freezer

CHOCOLATE JAM THUMBPRINTS

Traditionally, thumbprint cookies are nut-studded cakey clouds, each holding a drop of jam. Here, we've reinvented them to become chocolate walnut cookies—but still with that characteristic dab of jam.

MAKES A LITTLE LESS THAN 3 DOZEN COOKIES

2	cups all-purpose flour
½	teaspoon salt
¼	teaspoon baking soda
18	tablespoons (2 sticks plus 2 tablespoons) cool, unsalted butter, cut into small pieces, plus additional for greasing the baking sheets
½	cup plus 2 tablespoons cocoa powder, preferably Dutch-processed, sifted
2	large egg whites
2	tablespoons room-temperature water
2¾	cups walnut pieces, finely ground (yielding about 2 cups)
½	cup granulated sugar
½	cup packed light brown sugar
2	large egg yolks, at room temperature
2	teaspoons vanilla extract
¾	cup cherry jam

1. Position the rack in the center of the oven; preheat the oven to 375°F. Lightly butter a large baking sheet and set aside.

2. First, whisk the flour, salt, and baking soda in a medium bowl until well combined; set aside. Melt 5 tablespoons of the butter in a microwave or a small saucepan set over low heat; cool a moment or two, then mix in the cocoa powder, stirring until a firm paste forms—set this mixture aside as well. Beat the egg whites with the water in a small bowl until frothy; set aside. Finally, place the ground walnuts on a large plate.

3. To make the dough, use an electric mixer at medium speed to soften the remaining butter (13 tablespoons, or 1 stick plus 5 tablespoons) in a large bowl. When it's smooth but still cool, add the granulated sugar and the brown sugar and beat until light, pale brown, and airy, a little less than 2 minutes. Beat in the egg yolks one at a time, then scrape down the sides of the bowl and beat in the vanilla until smooth.

4. Add the prepared chocolate paste; beat until smooth, about 1 minute at medium speed. Then remove the beaters and stir in the prepared flour mixture with a wooden spoon or a rubber spatula. The batter will be thick but quite soft. Stir only until the flour is incorporated, not until the batter starts to change color.

5. Scoop out a heaping tablespoon of the dough and roll it into a 1-inch ball. Roll this ball in the egg-white mixture, then in the ground nuts. Place on the prepared baking sheet and continue making nut-coated balls, spacing them about 1½ inches apart on the sheet. Bake for 5 minutes.

6. Remove the baking sheet from the oven and press a thumbprint in the center of each cookie. Wet your thumb to protect it from the heat of the cookie, then gently but firmly press down into the cookie, first straight down, then nudging and bending your thumb until it flattens somewhat, thereby creating a well and cracking the sides of the cookie. Do not press through to the baking sheet. Alternatively, you can use the handle of a wooden spoon to make this indentation, although you might have to move it around to get a well the size of your thumbprint. Fill each indent with 1 teaspoon cherry jam.

7. Bake for about 10 more minutes, or until the cookies are firm to the touch. Cool on the baking sheet for 2 minutes, then transfer to a wire rack to cool completely. Cool the baking sheet for 5 minutes and butter it a second time before proceeding with additional batches—or use a second buttered baking sheet that hasn't already been in the oven.

Make It Your Own!

This cookie has endless variations, achieved simply by altering the jam used, from blueberry to strawberry rhubarb, from grape to orange marmalade. And don't neglect exotic or unusual jams, like Damson plum or gooseberry. We do not recommend using jelly or preserves—you need the thickness of jams without the large chunks sometimes found in preserves.

You can also substitute other nuts for the walnuts in the coating. We suggest an equivalent amount of hazelnuts or pecans.

CHOCOLATE LACE
SANDWICH COOKIES

These traditional cookies are perhaps a little out of vogue now, but well deserve a comeback. They're thin and crisp, like a crackly caramel dotted with chopped cashews, sandwiching a thin layer of melted chocolate.

MAKES ABOUT 40 COOKIES

¼ cup all-purpose flour

½ teaspoon baking soda

⅛ teaspoon salt

6 tablespoons cool, unsalted butter, cut into small pieces

¼ cup packed dark brown sugar

2 tablespoons granulated sugar

1 tablespoon corn syrup

1 large egg yolk, at room temperature

1 teaspoon vanilla extract

½ cup finely chopped, plain, roasted cashews (do not use salted cashews)

6 ounces semisweet chocolate, chopped

1. Position the racks in the top and bottom thirds of the oven; preheat the oven to 375°F. Line two large baking sheets with parchment paper or silicone baking mats; set aside. Whisk the flour, baking soda, and salt in a medium bowl until well combined; set aside as well.

2. Soften the butter in a large bowl, using an electric mixer at medium speed. Add the dark brown sugar, granulated sugar, and corn syrup; continue beating until light but still a little grainy, about 1 minute. Beat in the egg yolk, then the vanilla. Remove the beaters, add the prepared flour mixture and cashews all at once, and stir with a wooden spoon or a rubber spatula just until incorporated. You should have a soft, wet batter that holds its shape.

3. Scoop up ½ teaspoon of the batter and drop it on one of the prepared baking sheets. Continue making small mounds, spacing them about 2 inches apart on both sheets.

4. Bake for 4 minutes, then rotate the sheets top to bottom and back to front. Bake for about 4 more minutes, or until the cookies are flat and browned; they should also have small lacy holes and thin slits. Don't overbake—the cookies will be very soft, pliable, and fragile. Cool on the sheets for 15 minutes, or until the cookies are firm and can be peeled off the parchment or silicone baking mats. Transfer to a wire rack and cool completely. If you have more batter for more cookies, let the sheets cool another 10 minutes before proceeding. When done, you'll have made about 80 cookies.

5. When the cookies are cool, place the chocolate in the top half of a double boiler set over about 1 inch of simmering water, or in a bowl that fits tightly over a medium saucepan with a similar amount of simmering water. Be careful of any escaping steam—it can burn you or cause the chocolate to seize. Stir until half the chocolate has melted, then remove the top half of the double boiler or the bowl from the heat and continue stirring until all the chocolate has melted. Transfer to a clean, dry bowl and set aside to cool for 5 minutes.

6. Use a pastry brush to paint a thick but shiny coating of chocolate on the bottom of one of the lacy cookies, then sandwich that chocolate layer against the bottom of a second cookie, thereby creating a lacy sandwich. Continue making lacy sandwiches with the rest of the cookies. Set them on a wire rack to cool for about 30 minutes, or until the chocolate has hardened.

Recommended storage
3 days at room temperature between sheets of parchment paper
Not recommended for freezing

More Choices!
These cookies are equally good substituting ½ cup finely chopped unsalted macadamia nuts for the cashews. You can also use 6 ounces milk chocolate or white chocolate instead of the semisweet chocolate.

CHOCOLATE LINZER COOKIES

An Austrian specialty, Linzer tarts are nut pastry-crusts sandwiching a thin layer of raspberry jam. Here, we've reinterpreted that classic, turning it into a chocolate cookie: the dough is made from ground walnuts, not the traditional almonds, but a better match for the chocolate; and we've sandwiched the cookies around a smooth, creamy, ganache-like icing. If you miss the raspberry jam, simply forgo the cocoa-powder coating and serve them with a dab of jam on top.

MAKES 15 LARGE SANDWICH COOKIES

FOR THE COOKIE DOUGH

2	cups plus 2 tablespoons all-purpose flour, plus additional for dusting
½	teaspoon baking powder
½	teaspoon ground cinnamon
½	teaspoon salt
8	tablespoons (1 stick) cool, unsalted butter, cut into small pieces
¼	cup solid vegetable shortening (2 ounces)
¾	cup sugar
1	large egg, at room temperature
½	teaspoon finely grated orange zest
1½	cups walnut pieces, finely ground

FOR THE FILLING

6	ounces semisweet chocolate, chopped
⅓	cup heavy cream
8	tablespoons (1 stick) unsalted butter, softened (see Note)
2	cups confectioners' sugar

FOR THE COATING

2	tablespoons confectioners' sugar
1	tablespoon cocoa powder, sifted

1. Position the racks in the top and bottom thirds of the oven; preheat the oven to 325°F. Line two large baking sheets with parchment paper or silicone baking mats;

set aside. Whisk the flour, baking powder, cinnamon, and salt in a medium bowl until well combined; set aside as well.

2. Soften the butter and shortening in a large bowl, using an electric mixer at medium speed, just until creamy, if still cool, about 1 minute. Add the sugar and beat the mixture at medium speed until light and fluffy, about 1 more minute. Beat in the egg and orange zest until smooth, then the ground walnuts, just until incorporated.

3. Turn off the mixer, pour in the prepared flour mixture, and beat at a very low speed just until a soft, pliable dough forms. Gather the dough into a ball in the bowl; divide this ball into thirds and cover with a kitchen towel.

4. Lightly dust a clean, dry work surface with flour. Place one-third of the dough on it, flatten slightly, dust with flour, and roll out to an even ¼-inch thickness. Cut the dough into large 3-inch circles using a cookie cutter or a similarly shaped drinking glass dusted with flour. The cookies will be very soft; transfer them gently with a large metal spatula to the prepared baking sheets, spacing them about 1½ inches apart.

5. Gather any scraps, add to the second third of the dough, and roll out as directed. Using these two balls of dough, and any scraps, cut out fifteen 3-inch circles.

6. Dust your work surface again with flour, place the last third of the dough on it, and roll out to the same thickness, about ¼ inch thick. Cut out 3-inch cookies, but before lifting them off the work surface, use a 1-inch-diameter circular cookie cutter or a very small drinking glass, dusted with flour, to cut a center hole out of each circle. Gather all scraps and roll again until you have 15 tops with circles cut out of their centers. Use a large metal spatula to transfer these to the prepared baking sheets as well. (If you cannot fit them all onto two baking sheets, cover these cut-out tops with a clean kitchen towel and reserve them for a second baking on a lined baking sheet.)

7. Bake for 8 minutes, then rotate the sheets top to bottom and front to back. Bake for about 8 or 9 more minutes, just until the cookies begin to brown at the edges and are dry and set. One warning: the tops will bake more quickly than the bottoms, so watch them carefully. Cool for 2 minutes on the sheets, then use a wire spatula to transfer to wire racks to cool completely, about 1 hour.

8. To make the filling, place the chopped chocolate in a medium bowl. Heat the cream in a small saucepan set over medium-low heat until small bubbles form around the rim of the pan. Pour this warmed cream over the chocolate and stir with a wooden spoon or heat-safe rubber spatula until all the chocolate has melted.

9. In a second bowl, cream the butter and confectioners' sugar, using an electric mixer at medium speed. With the beaters running, pour in the melted chocolate mixture in a thin, slow, steady stream, scraping down the sides of the bowl as necessary.

10. Use an offset spatula or a long, thin spatula to frost what will become the bottom of the cookies—that is, the cookies that don't have a hole cut in their centers. Mound 2 tablespoons of ganache in the center of the cookie, then pull it toward the rim on all sides, leaving the heaviest layer of ganache in the center. Top with one of the cut-out cookie tops, letting the mounds poke through the hole. Set the sandwiched cookies on a wire rack so the chocolate will harden, about 1 hour.

11. Finally, make a dusted coating for the cookies by mixing the confectioners' sugar and cocoa powder in a small bowl or teacup until uniform. Dust this mixture over the filled cookie sandwiches.

NOTE: *The butter for this ganache-like filling is not beaten for structure, but for texture—therefore, the rule about cool butter for batters does not apply here. The butter should be quite soft.*

Recommended storage
2 days at room temperature between sheets of wax paper
Not recommended for freezing when sandwiched; the cookies alone can be stored in the freezer for up to 3 months, then filled and dusted when thawed

Mix It Up!

Chocolate Mint Linzer Cookies: Omit the ground cinnamon and the orange zest. Add ½ teaspoon mint extract with the egg.

Chocolate Orange Linzer Cookies: Omit the ground cinnamon. Reduce the cream to ¼ cup. Add 1½ tablespoons frozen orange juice concentrate, thawed, with the remaining cream.

Chocolate Raspberry Linzer Cookies: Omit the ground cinnamon. Reduce the cream to ¼ cup. Add 1½ tablespoons raspberry liqueur, such as Chambord, with the remaining cream.

Chocolate Rum Linzer Cookies: Omit the orange zest. Add 1 teaspoon rum extract with the egg. Reduce the cream to ¼ cup. Add 1½ tablespoons dark rum with the remaining cream.

CHOCOLATE MADELEINES

Madeleines ride the line between cookies and cake. Although they're treated like a cookie—served a couple at a time and often in the middle of the day with coffee or tea—they have the crumby springy texture of a sponge cake. You'll need a madeleine pan to make these French treats; for best results, choose either a flexible silicone pan or a nonstick pan with indentations about 3 inches long and 2 inches wide.

MAKES ABOUT 2½ DOZEN COOKIES

Nonstick spray (see Note)
1¼	cups all-purpose flour
¼	cup cocoa powder, preferably Dutch-processed, sifted
½	teaspoon baking powder
¼	teaspoon salt
12	tablespoons (1½ sticks) cool, unsalted butter, cut into small pieces
1¼	cups confectioners' sugar
3	large eggs, at room temperature
1	tablespoon milk (regular, low-fat, or nonfat)
1	teaspoon vanilla extract

1. Position the rack in the center of the oven; preheat the oven to 350°F. Lightly spray the madeleine pan with nonstick spray; set aside. Whisk the flour, cocoa powder, baking powder, and salt in a medium bowl until the mixture is evenly colored; set aside as well.

2. Soften the butter in a large bowl, using an electric mixer at medium speed, about 1 minute. Add the confectioners' sugar and continue beating until light and fluffy, about 1 more minute. Beat in the eggs one at time, making sure each is thoroughly incorporated before adding the next. Then beat in the milk and vanilla. Remove the beaters and use a rubber spatula to fold in the prepared flour mixture just until moistened and incorporated. Do not overmix—the batter will still be grainy with flour although no dry, white streaks should be visible.

3. Fill the indentations in the prepared madeleine pan with 1 tablespoon of the batter. Use the back of a flatware spoon to spread the batter gently in the indentation, pressing down slightly to create a concave surface in each cookie (this will keep it from rising too much and puffing up).

4. Bake for 12 minutes, reversing the pan back to front halfway through baking. The madeleines should be set but springy to the touch. Cool in the pan for 1 minute, then turn the pan over on a wire rack to release the madeleines. Place them, smooth side down, on the rack and cool completely. Cool the pan for 5 minutes before lightly spraying it again and baking additional madeleines.

NOTE: *We don't recommend using butter to grease the pan because you want a very thin coating—the madeleines must not fry as they bake. Lightly grease the pan, even if it has a nonstick surface, because the coating will put a barrier between the chocolate and the heat, thereby ensuring that the chocolate at the madeleines' edges doesn't singe and turn bitter.*

Recommended storage
3 days at room temperature
2 months in the freezer

More Choices!

Chocolate Chip Madeleines: Mix in ¾ cup mini chocolate chips after the milk.

Chocolate Currant Madeleines: Mix in ¾ cup currants after the milk.

Chocolate Orange Madeleines: Substitute 1 tablespoon finely grated orange zest and ½ teaspoon orange extract for the vanilla extract.

CHOCOLATE MANDELBROT

Sometimes called "Jewish biscotti," mandelbrot ("mandel" = almonds; "brot" = bread) are dry cookies, often served after a holiday meal. Our version fills this traditional cookie with a rich vein of chocolate. The dough is soft, almost like a yeast dough; so the cookies are softer and moister than Italian biscotti.

MAKES ABOUT 4 DOZEN COOKIES

½	cup almond paste (about 4 ounces, see page 17)
1½	cups sugar
½	teaspoon salt
11	tablespoons (1 stick plus 3 tablespoons) cool, unsalted butter, cut into small pieces
5	large eggs, at room temperature
1	teaspoon vanilla extract
½	teaspoon almond extract
3	cups all-purpose flour, plus additional for dusting
1	cup cocoa powder, sifted
¼	cup hot water
2	tablespoons cool water

1. Position the rack in the center of the oven; preheat the oven to 375°F. Line a large baking sheet with parchment paper; set aside.

2. Cut the almond paste into 1 cup of the sugar and the salt in a large bowl, using a pastry cutter or two forks, until the mixture resembles coarse meal. Add the butter and continue cutting in a few turns, just until softened a little. Then beat with an electric mixer at medium speed until light and fluffy, about 2 minutes.

3. Beat in 4 of the eggs at medium speed, one at a time, scraping down the sides of the bowl as necessary. Then beat in the vanilla and almond extract until smooth. Finally, beat in the flour in ½-cup increments at very low speed just until a soft dough forms. There's a fine line here between cookies and bread—you want a soft dough that's not sticky. When in doubt, beat less than you might think necessary.

4. Lightly dust a dry work surface with flour and turn the dough onto it. Knead for about 2 minutes, just until the flour has been incorporated and the dough is smooth. Divide in half, lightly flour your work surface and the dough, and roll or press each half into a 12 × 6-inch rectangle. Cover with clean kitchen towels.

5. In a medium bowl, mix the cocoa powder, hot water, and the remaining ½ cup sugar to form a thick, smooth paste. A fork works best—the mixture will be stiff. Divide this chocolate paste in half and make a flattened log about 11 inches long out of each half. Place this log in the middle of each half of the rolled-out dough, allowing about ½ inch on each end. Fold the almond dough over and around the chocolate log; pinch to seal the seam and both ends, taking care not to leave gaps in the seals. Place these filled logs, seam side down, on the prepared baking sheet, about 4 inches apart.

6. Beat the remaining egg with the cool water, then brush this mixture over each loaf on the sheet, using a pastry brush or pastry feather.

7. Bake for 45 minutes, rotating the sheet front to back once halfway through baking, until the logs are very brown and firm to the touch. Cool completely on the baking sheet, about 1 hour. Lower the oven temperature to 325°F.

8. Remove the logs from the baking sheet and use a serrated knife to slice them into ½-inch pieces. If desired, slice them on the diagonal for longer slices. Return these slices to the parchment-lined baking sheet, placing them cut side down. If you need to use a second baking sheet, line it with parchment paper as well—but toast the cookies one sheet at a time.

9. Bake for 10 minutes, turn the cookies over to the other cut side, and bake for another 10 minutes, or until lightly toasted. Cool for 5 minutes on the baking sheet, then transfer the cookies to a wire rack to cool completely.

Recommended storage
5 days at room temperature between sheets of wax paper
3 months in the freezer

CHOCOLATE MARSHMALLOW COOKIES

Here's our interpretation of Mallomars: a crisp cookie with a marshmallow set on top, covered in a chocolate shell.

MAKES ABOUT 3 DOZEN SMALL COOKIES

1	cup plus 3 tablespoons all-purpose flour
¼	teaspoon baking powder
¼	teaspoon salt
4	tablespoons (½ stick) cool, unsalted butter, cut into small pieces
¼	cup solid vegetable shortening (2 ounces)
½	cup plus 1 tablespoon sugar
2	tablespoons honey
1	large egg yolk, at room temperature
1	teaspoon vanilla extract
1	cup graham cracker crumbs (see Note)
18	large marshmallows
12	ounces semisweet or bittersweet chocolate, chopped

1. Whisk the flour, baking powder, and salt in a medium bowl until well combined; set aside.

2. Soften the butter and shortening in a large bowl, using an electric mixer at medium speed, about 1 minute. Add the sugar and beat the mixture until fluffy and light, about 1 more minute. Beat in the honey, scrape down the sides of the bowl, and beat in the egg yolk and vanilla. Continue beating until airy and light, about 30 seconds.

3. Remove the electric beaters and stir in the graham cracker crumbs with a wooden spoon or rubber spatula. Then stir in the prepared flour mixture just until incorporated. The batter will be very soft but will hold together. Form it into a ball, wrap in plastic wrap, flatten into a thick disk, seal, and place in the refrigerator until firm but not rock hard, about 1 hour, but not more than 3 hours.

4. Meanwhile, position the rack in the center of the oven and preheat the oven to 350°F.

5. When firm, divide the dough in half; flatten each half a bit. Place each half between two fresh sheets of plastic wrap; lay one piece of dough on your work surface and return the other to the refrigerator. Roll the disk into a circle ¼ inch thick and 10 inches in diameter. Remove the top sheet of plastic wrap and cut the dough into small 1- or 1½-inch circles. If you cut carefully, you can use almost all the dough—but if you have leftovers, gather them together, cover with plastic wrap, and place back into the refrigerator for about 1 hour, then reroll as directed.

6. Use a metal spatula to transfer the cut-out circles to a large, ungreased baking sheet, preferably nonstick, spacing them about 1 inch apart. Bake for 8 to 10 minutes, or until lightly browned and somewhat springy to the touch.

7. While the cookies are baking, cut the marshmallows in half horizontally with kitchen scissors. You may need to clean the scissors as you cut the marshmallows to keep the residue from sticking to them and thus tearing other marshmallows as you cut them.

8. The moment the cookies come out of the oven, while they're still hot and on the baking sheet, place one cut marshmallow disk sticky side down on each cookie, so that the marshmallow begins to soften. Once all the cookies are topped, go over them all again, pressing down slightly so that the marshmallow mushes to the edges of the cookie. Cool the cookies completely on the baking sheet.

9. Repeat with the second batch of dough: rolling it out, cutting it into disks, baking them, and topping with marshmallows.

10. Once all the cookies are cool, place the chocolate in the top half of a double boiler set over about 1 inch of boiling water, or in a medium bowl that fits snugly over a medium pot with about the same amount of simmering water. Stir until half the chocolate has melted, taking care not to let any steam get into the melting chocolate. Remove the top half of the double boiler or the bowl from the heat and continue stirring until all the chocolate has melted. Transfer to a deep bowl to create a pool of chocolate, then cool for 5 minutes.

11. Lay a large sheet of plastic wrap on your work surface, then set a wire rack on top of the plastic wrap. Pick up one cookie and dip it marshmallow side down into the melted chocolate, letting the chocolate come up to the crisp cookie and cover its sides but not the bottom. Pull the cookie up, gently shake any excess chocolate back into the bowl, and place the cookie marshmallow side up on the wire rack. Repeat with the remaining cookies. Let stand for about 1 hour, perhaps 90 minutes, to harden.

NOTE: *If you're not using purchased graham cracker crumbs, pulse 8 whole graham crackers in a food processor fitted with the chopping blade to make about 1 cup of crumbs. Do not use reduced-fat graham crackers for this recipe.*

Recommended storage
1 week at room temperature
Not recommended for freezing

Customize It!

Mix any one of the following into the melted chocolate: ½ cup unsweetened coconut chips; ½ cup Kellogg's Cocoa Rice Krispies or plain Rice Krispies cereal; ⅓ cup finely chopped pecans; ⅓ cup finely chopped, unsalted macadamia nuts; ⅓ cup finely chopped, unsalted, roasted peanuts; ⅓ cup finely chopped walnuts; ⅓ cup sliced almonds; 2 tablespoons finely chopped crystallized ginger; ½ teaspoon banana flavoring; or ¼ teaspoon ground cayenne pepper

The ingredients should be stirred in just after the chocolate has fully melted; make sure they are at room temperature to prevent the chocolate from seizing.

CHOCOLATE MELTIES

Melt-aways are American classics: little crescents made with lots of cornstarch for a crunch that instantly melts in your mouth. The fat in the chocolate causes the cookies to spread a little—but they still have that famous crunch. One tip: handle the dough as little as possible; even the natural oils on your hands will toughen the cookies.

MAKES A LITTLE MORE THAN 3 DOZEN COOKIES

½ pound (2 sticks) cool, unsalted butter, cut into small pieces

½ cup confectioners' sugar, plus more for dusting

2 teaspoons vanilla extract

1 cup cornstarch

¾ cup all-purpose flour

3 ounces semisweet chocolate, grated (about 1 cup, see Note)

1. Soften the butter in a large bowl, using an electric mixer at medium speed, about 1 minute. Add the confectioners' sugar and beat until creamy and light, about 1 more minute. Beat in the vanilla. Turn off the beaters, add the cornstarch and flour, and beat at a very low speed until soft and light, about 30 seconds. The dough will not necessarily hold together. Remove the beaters and gently fold in the grated chocolate, using a rubber spatula or a wooden spoon, just until evenly distributed in the batter. Cover the bowl with a clean kitchen towel and refrigerate for 2 hours, or until firm.

2. Position the racks in the top and bottom thirds of the oven; preheat the oven to 375°F.

3. Dust a clean, dry work surface lightly with confectioners' sugar. Divide the dough into 4 pieces. Knead 1 piece a few times, just to soften it a little—not too much or the chocolate will begin to melt. Roll into a log about 12 inches long and ½ inch in diameter, then slice into 1-inch pieces. (If your knife sticks, dust it with confectioners' sugar.) Place these cut pieces on a large, ungreased baking sheet, preferably nonstick, spacing them about 2 inches apart. If desired, gently bend them into crescents. Repeat this process with the other pieces of dough, filling two baking sheets with the sliced pieces of dough. Refrigerate any remaining dough for a second baking.

4. Bake for 6 minutes, then rotate the sheets back to front and top to bottom. Bake for an additional 6 minutes, or until soft but dry. The cookies will give a little but not spring back if touched—be careful: they are fragile. Cool for 5 minutes on the baking sheets, then transfer to wire racks to cool completely. Cool the baking sheets for 10 minutes before baking additional melties. Once all the cookies are completely cooled, dust them with confectioners' sugar if desired.

NOTE: *The best way to grate the chocolate for these cookies is with a vegetable peeler—run it quickly over the chocolate squares, creating thin shards, not long strips. You can also use the small holes of a box grater.*

Recommended storage
4 days at room temperature
Not recommended for freezing

Personalize It!

Melt 6 ounces of semisweet, bittersweet, or white chocolate; cool for 5 minutes. Lay a large sheet of wax paper under the rack holding the cooled cookies. Dip a fork into the melted chocolate and drizzle the chocolate over the cookies, waggling the fork in all directions to create a spider-web design over the cookies.

CHOCOLATE MERINGUE CAPS

These are a cookie version of chocolate meringue pie: soft, cakey cookies, topped with a light meringue cap and studded with almonds.

MAKES ABOUT 40 COOKIES

FOR THE COOKIES

2¼	cups all-purpose flour
1½	teaspoons baking powder
¼	teaspoon salt
6	ounces bittersweet chocolate, chopped (see Note)
8	tablespoons (1 stick) cool, unsalted butter, cut into small pieces, plus additional for greasing the baking sheets
½	cup packed light brown sugar
¼	cup granulated sugar
2	large egg yolks, at room temperature
1	teaspoon almond extract
¼	cup milk (regular or low-fat, but not nonfat)

FOR THE MERINGUE

2	large egg whites, at room temperature
⅛	teaspoon salt
½	cup superfine sugar (see page 21)
1	tablespoon all-purpose flour
1	cup sliced almonds

1. Position the racks in the top and bottom thirds of the oven. Preheat the oven to 375°F.

2. To make the cookies, butter two large baking sheets and set them aside. Mix the flour, baking powder, and salt in a medium bowl; set aside as well.

3. Place the chocolate in the top half of a double boiler set over about 1 inch of simmering water, or in a medium bowl that fits tightly over a medium saucepan with a similar amount of simmering water. Stir until half the chocolate has melted, adjusting the heat as necessary to have a smooth, low simmer and taking care not to let any of the escaping steam condense into the melting chocolate. Remove the top half of the double boiler or the bowl from the heat and continue stirring until the chocolate has completely melted. Set aside to cool for 5 minutes.

4. In the meantime, soften the butter in a large bowl, using an electric mixer at medium speed, about 1 minute. Add the brown sugar and granulated sugar and continue beating until fluffy and light, about 1 more minute. Beat in the egg yolks one at a time, then beat in the almond extract until smooth.

5. With the mixer running at low speed, slowly pour in the melted, cooled chocolate. Scrape down the sides of the bowl as necessary and beat just until smooth. Turn off the mixer, add half the prepared flour mixture, then beat at low speed until smooth. Pour in the milk and beat for 10 seconds. Remove the beaters and fold in the remaining flour mixture with a rubber spatula just until a soft dough forms. Set aside while you prepare the meringue.

6. Scrupulously clean and dry the beaters, then place the egg whites and salt in a clean, dry, room-temperature bowl and beat at high speed until soft peaks form. Add the sugar slowly in 1-tablespoon increments and continue beating until the mixture forms firm, thick, satiny peaks. Remove the beaters and fold in the flour with a rubber spatula, taking care not to deflate the beaten whites. Gently fold in the almonds, just until evenly distributed in the batter.

7. Roll a heaping teaspoonful of the chocolate dough into a ball, place it on one of the prepared baking sheets, and gently press the ball with your fingers into a circle about 2 inches in diameter. Continue making these flattened disks, spacing them about 2 inches apart on the sheets. Top each disk with 1 teaspoon of meringue, gently spreading it to the edges of the cookie with the back of a spoon. Mound the meringue in the middle of each disk, creating a small cap on the cookie. Seal the edges of the meringue to the cookie by pressing lightly with a finger.

8. Bake for 7 minutes, then rotate the trays top to bottom and back to front. Bake for another 7 or 8 minutes, or until the meringue is light brown and dry to the touch. Cool on the sheets for 1 minute, then transfer the cookies to wire racks to cool completely. Cool the baking sheets at least 5 minutes and butter them again before baking further batches.

NOTE: *If you substitute semisweet chocolate, increase the chopped chocolate to 7 ounces and decrease the granulated sugar to 3 tablespoons plus 1 teaspoon.*

Recommended storage
3 days at room temperature
Not recommended for freezing

More Choices!

Chocolate Cocoa Meringue Caps: Fold in 1 tablespoon cocoa powder, sifted, to the meringue filling with the flour.

Chocolate Coconut Meringue Caps: Substitute 1¼ cups unsweetened coconut chips for the almonds.

Chocolate Pecan Meringue Caps: Substitute 1 cup chopped pecans for the almonds.

Chocolate Walnut Meringue Caps: Substitute 1 cup chopped walnuts for the almonds.

CHOCOLATE MERINGUES

ook no further for the ultimate chocolate meringues. These cookies are best on the second day, as the chocolate flavor intensifies overnight. Don't forget to serve something to dunk them in: milk, tea, or a dessert wine.

MAKES ABOUT 2½ DOZEN MERINGUES

- ¾ cup superfine sugar (see page 21)
- 6 tablespoons cocoa powder, preferably natural, sifted
- 3 large egg whites, at room temperature
- ⅛ teaspoon salt
- ⅛ teaspoon cream of tartar
- 2 teaspoons vanilla extract
- ½ cup mini chocolate chips
- ½ cup ground walnuts

1. Position the rack in the center of the oven. Preheat the oven to 250°F. Line a large baking sheet with parchment paper; set aside. Mix the sugar and cocoa powder together in a medium bowl; set aside as well.

2. Beat the egg whites and salt in a large, dry bowl with an electric mixer at medium speed until frothy. Add the cream of tartar, increase the speed to high, and beat until soft peaks form. With the beaters at high speed, add in the sugar mixture 1 tablespoon at a time; beat each addition for about 15 seconds. Once all the sugar mixture has been added, continue beating until shiny, firm peaks form; you should be able to feel no grains of sugar between your fingers if you take a pinch of the mixture.

3. Gently fold in the mini chocolate chips and ground walnuts with a rubber spatula, taking care not to deflate the egg whites—use slow, sweeping arcs; fold just until they are mixed evenly in the batter. Drop by rounded teaspoonfuls onto the prepared baking sheet.

4. Bake for 1½ hours, rotating the sheet back to front once halfway through. The meringues should be quite dry; you should be able to pull one off the parchment easily. Let them cool completely on the baking sheet before removing them.

Recommended storage
1 week at room temperature
Not recommended for freezing

Mix It Up!

Chocolate M&M Meringues: Substitute M&M's Mini Baking Bits for the mini chocolate chips.

Mint Chocolate Meringues: Chop ½ cup mint chocolate chips into small pieces, then substitute them for the mini chocolate chips.

CHOCOLATE MINT MARBLE REFRIGERATOR COOKIES

These flat disks look like little chips of marble and taste something like a mint variation of the classic chocolate butter cookie. Best of all, you can make the dough ahead and keep it in the refrigerator for up to 5 days, slicing off and baking as many cookies as you want at any one time.

MAKES A FEW MORE THAN 3 DOZEN COOKIES

- ½ pound (2 sticks) cool, unsalted butter, cut into small pieces
- ⅔ cup plus 3 tablespoons granulated sugar
- ½ teaspoon salt
- 2 large egg yolks, at room temperature
- 1⅓ cups plus 2 tablespoons all-purpose flour
- ¼ cup cocoa powder, preferably natural, sifted
- 1 teaspoon vanilla extract
- 1 teaspoon red food coloring
- ¼ cup confectioners' sugar
- 1 teaspoon mint extract
- 3 drops green food coloring

1. Soften the butter in a large bowl, using an electric mixer at medium speed. Add ⅔ cup of the sugar and the salt; continue beating until smooth and light, about 2 minutes. Beat in the egg yolks one at a time; then remove the beaters and use a wooden spoon or a rubber spatula to stir in 1⅓ cups of the flour until a soft, creamy batter forms. Divide the dough in half, placing it in two medium bowls.

2. Into one half of the dough, stir in the cocoa powder, vanilla, and red food coloring as well as the remaining 3 tablespoons sugar. In the other half, stir the confectioners' sugar, mint extract, and green food coloring as well as the remaining 2 tablespoons flour. Cover both bowls and refrigerate until both doughs are firm enough to roll out, about 1 hour.

3. Divide each of the doughs into 8 pieces (so you have 16 pieces of dough). Shape about half of these into short logs about 2 inches thick. Gently pat the remainder into circles, ovals, or rectangles. The point is to have many shapes and sizes of dough to fuse together. Lay these out on your work surface, with some of the pieces overlapping, some of them sticking up, and others lying on their sides, greens and reds mixed together. Starting at one long side of this mass of shapes, use your hands to roll them all together into a large log, about 11 inches long and 2½ inches in diameter. Wrap this log in plastic wrap, evening out its shape through the wrap. Seal well and refrigerate for at least 4 hours, or up to 5 days.

4. Position the rack in the center of the oven; preheat the oven to 350°F. Slice the log into ¼-inch-thick disks and place them on a large, ungreased baking sheet, preferably nonstick, spacing the disks about 1½ inches apart.

5. Bake for about 15 minutes, rotating the sheet back to front once during baking, until the cookies are browned at the edges and are firm to the touch, if still a bit springy. Cool for 3 minutes on the baking sheet, then transfer the cookies to a wire rack to cool completely. Cool the baking sheet for 5 minutes before baking additional cookies.

Recommended storage
5 days at room temperature
3 months in the freezer after baking

More Choices!

Chocolate Almond Marble Refrigerator Cookies: Omit the green food coloring. Substitute almond extract for the mint extract.

Chocolate Banana Marble Refrigerator Cookies: Substitute yellow food coloring for the green; substitute banana flavoring for the mint extract.

Chocolate Orange Marble Refrigerator Cookies: Substitute orange food coloring for the green; substitute orange extract for the mint extract.

Chocolate Rum Marble Refrigerator Cookies: Omit the green food coloring. Substitute rum extract for the mint extract.

CHOCOLATE MINT SANDWICH COOKIES

Here's a cookie that replicates Mint Milanos, the fix of every midnight snacker, the bane of every dieter. Why make your own? For the sheer fun of it, of course. These tender water cookies taste a little like a vanilla wafer. They're good on their own, but isn't the chocolate-mint filling always the best part?

MAKES ABOUT 1 DOZEN LARGE SANDWICH COOKIES

4	tablespoons solid vegetable shortening (2 ounces), plus additional for greasing the baking sheet
⅔	cup sugar
1	large egg, at room temperature
2	large egg whites, at room temperature, lightly beaten with a fork
2	teaspoons vanilla extract
¾	cup all-purpose flour, plus additional for the baking sheet
2½	ounces semisweet chocolate, chopped
1½	tablespoons crème de menthe or mint syrup
⅛	teaspoon peppermint oil (optional)

1. Position the rack in the center of the oven; preheat the oven to 425°F. Use a dab of shortening on a small piece of wax paper to grease a large baking sheet; flour the baking sheet, then set it aside.

2. Beat the shortening and sugar in a large bowl, using an electric mixer at medium speed, until light and airy, about 1 minute. Beat in the egg, then beat in the egg whites in two increments, making sure the first is thoroughly incorporated before adding the second. Beat in the vanilla until smooth. Remove the beaters and stir in the flour, using a wooden spoon or a rubber spatula, just until incorporated.

3. Fit a pastry bag with a round, ¾-inch tip; fill the bag with the dough, squeezing it toward the tip. Pipe out twenty-four 3-inch-long cookies on to the prepared baking sheet, each about as thick as your thumb. Space the cookies about 2 inches apart on the sheet. (If the baking sheet is not large enough to accommodate all the cookies, reserve some of the dough for a second baking.)

4. Bake for 8 to 10 minutes until set and very lightly browned at the edges but still springy to the touch. Cool the cookies on the baking sheet for 2 minutes, then use a metal spatula to transfer them gently to a wire rack to cool completely.

5. Once the cookies have cooled, place the chocolate in the top half of a double boiler set over about 1 inch of simmering water, or in a medium bowl that fits snugly over a medium saucepan with a similar amount of simmering water. Stir until half the chocolate has melted, then remove the top half of the double boiler or the bowl from the heat and continue stirring until the chocolate has fully melted. Transfer to a clean bowl and let stand for 10 minutes to cool almost to room temperature. Stir in the crème de menthe or mint syrup, and the peppermint oil, if using, until smooth.

6. Spread a scant 2 teaspoons of the chocolate-mint mixture on the flat side of one of the cookies, taking care to smooth it to the sides. Gently top with a second cookie, flat side down. Set on the wire rack until the chocolate hardens, about 1 hour. Repeat with the remaining filling and cookies.

Recommended storage
3 days at room temperature
Not recommended for freezing

Customize It!

You can endlessly vary the filling of these tender, light cookies. Omit the peppermint oil. Substitute any one of the following for the crème de menthe: raspberry liqueur, such as Chambord; almond liqueur, such as amaretto; apple schnapps; bitter orange liqueur, such as Mandarine Napoléon; cherry liqueur, such as Cherry Heering; chocolate liqueur, such as Godiva Liqueur; coffee liqueur, such as Kahlúa; Cognac; hazelnut liqueur, such as Frangelico; honey liqueur, such as Bärenjäger; or licorice liqueur, such as Sambuca.

CHOCOLATE MOLASSES RAISIN COOKIES

These cookies pack a triple punch of molasses, oatmeal, and chocolate. To make these soft, decadent cookies successfully, you'll need to take them out of the oven before you think they're done, when they're still a bit gooey to the touch. Too long in the oven and they turn hard—which defeats the point of these luscious, soft, homemade treats.

MAKES ABOUT 5 DOZEN COOKIES

1½	cups all-purpose flour
½	cup cocoa powder, sifted
2	teaspoons baking soda
1	teaspoon ground cinnamon
½	teaspoon salt
8	tablespoons (1 stick) cold, unsalted butter, cut into small pieces, plus additional for greasing the baking sheets
2	tablespoons solid vegetable shortening (1 ounce)
¾	cup sugar
¼	cup molasses, preferably unsulphured
1	large egg, at room temperature
1	cup raisins

1. Position the rack in the center of the oven; preheat the oven to 350°F. Lightly butter a large baking sheet; set aside. Mix the flour, cocoa powder, baking soda, cinnamon, and salt in a medium bowl until a uniform color; set aside as well.

2. Beat the butter and shortening in a large bowl, using an electric mixer at medium speed, until soft and smooth, about 1 minute. Scrape down the sides of the bowl, add the sugar and molasses, and continue beating until light, about 2 more minutes. Beat in the egg until smooth. Remove the beaters.

3. Stir in the prepared flour mixture with a wooden spoon or a rubber spatula. Do not overmix—just moisten the flour. Stir in the raisins until you have a soft, drop-cookie dough with no lumps, but with some grains of flour still visible.

4. Drop by rounded teaspoonfuls onto the prepared baking sheet, spacing the mounds about 1½ inches apart. Bake for 10 minutes, or until the tops appear dry and somewhat cracked but the insides are still quite soft. Cool on the baking sheet for 5 minutes, then transfer to a wire rack to cool completely. Cool the baking sheet for 5 minutes and butter it again to make another batch—or use a second buttered baking sheet that hasn't been in the oven.

Recommended storage
4 days at room temperature
2 months in the freezer

Customize It!
Omit the raisins and substitute 1 cup of any of the following, or a combination, in their place: chopped dates, chopped dried apricots, chopped dried figs, chopped dried pears, chopped dried strawberries, dried blueberries, dried cherries, or dried cranberries.

CHOCOLATE OATMEAL RAISIN COOKIES

hese chocolate cookies are made with oats and raisins mixed right into the dough. If you're looking for chewy chocolate chip oatmeal cookies, see the Soft Chocolate Chip Oatmeal Cookies (page 209). The cookies need a little mothering as they bake—but the results are more intense than traditional oatmeal cookies and quite fudgy.

MAKES ABOUT 3 DOZEN COOKIES

½	cup all-purpose flour
½	teaspoon baking soda
½	teaspoon salt
6	ounces semisweet chocolate, chopped
6	tablespoons cool, unsalted butter, cut into small pieces, plus additional for buttering the baking sheets
½	cup granulated sugar
½	cup packed dark brown sugar
1	large egg, at room temperature
1	teaspoon vanilla extract
2	cups rolled oats (do not use quick-cooking oats)
1½	cups raisins

1. Position the racks in the top and bottom thirds of the oven; preheat the oven to 350°F. Lightly butter two large baking sheets; set aside. Whisk the flour, baking soda, and salt in a medium bowl and set aside as well.

2. Place the chopped chocolate in the top half of a double boiler set over about an inch of simmering water, or in a medium bowl that fits tightly over a medium saucepan without about the same amount of simmering water. Stir until half the chocolate melts, taking care not to let any steam condense into the chocolate. Remove from the heat and continue stirring until the chocolate has completely melted. Set aside for 5 minutes to cool.

3. Soften the butter in a large bowl, using an electric mixer at medium speed, about 1 minute. Add both kinds of sugar and continue beating until light and fluffy, about 2 minutes. Beat in the egg and vanilla, then the melted, cooled chocolate until smooth. Turn off the mixer, add the prepared flour mixture, and beat at a very low speed just until incorporated. Use a wooden spoon to stir in the oats and raisins just until evenly distributed.

4. Drop by heaping teaspoonfuls onto the prepared baking sheets, spacing the mounds about 2 inches apart. Bake for 6 minutes, then rotate the sheets top to bottom and front to back. Continue baking for 4 more minutes. At this point, use a heat-safe rubber spatula or the back of a tablespoon to flatten the cookies slightly—just press down and make them more traditionally shaped. Continue baking for about 2 more minutes, or until the cookies have a somewhat firm, filmy crust on their tops, much like the layer of dried sand along the tidal shoreline of a beach, but the cookies themselves are still quite soft to the touch. Cool on the sheets for 5 minutes, then transfer to wire racks to cool completely. Cool the sheets for 5 more minutes and lightly butter them again before baking additional batches.

Recommended storage
4 days at room temperature between sheets of wax paper
3 months in the freezer

More Choices!

Chocolate Oatmeal Apricot Pistachio Cookies: Substitute ¾ cup chopped dried apricots and ¾ cup chopped unsalted pistachios for the raisins.

Chocolate Oatmeal Cranberry Almond Cookies: Substitute ¾ cup dried cranberries and ¾ cup slivered almonds for the raisins.

Chocolate Oatmeal Date Pecan Cookies: Substitute ¾ cup chopped pitted dates and ¾ cup chopped pecan pieces for the raisins.

Chocolate Oatmeal Raisin Cashew Cookies: Reduce the raisins to ¾ cup; add ¾ cup chopped roasted unsalted cashews with the remaining raisins.

Chocolate Oatmeal Raisin Walnut Cookies: Reduce the raisins to ¾ cup; add ¾ cup chopped walnut pieces with the remaining raisins.

CHOCOLATE PEANUT BUTTER BULL'S-EYES

You'll need to make two doughs for these colorful cookies: the chocolate part is rich and sweet; the peanut butter part is soft, creamy and a little salty. You create a bull's-eye out of the two doughs by rolling them into incrementally smaller balls, flattening them out, and setting them on top of each other. Sure, it requires a little effort—but the results are sure to be a hit.

MAKES ABOUT 45 COOKIES

FOR THE CHOCOLATE DOUGH

3	ounces unsweetened chocolate, chopped
12	tablespoons (1½ sticks) cool, unsalted butter, cut into small pieces
1	cup plus 2 tablespoons granulated sugar
1	large egg, at room temperature
1	large egg white, at room temperature
1½	teaspoons vanilla extract
¼	teaspoon salt
1¾	cups plus 2 tablespoons all-purpose flour

FOR THE PEANUT BUTTER DOUGH

6	tablespoons creamy peanut butter (do not use "natural" peanut butter)
4	tablespoons (½ stick) cool, unsalted butter, cut into small pieces
¾	cup packed light brown sugar
1	large egg yolk, at room temperature
¼	cup plus 2 tablespoons all-purpose flour
¼	teaspoon salt

1. First, position the rack in the middle of the oven. Preheat the oven to 350°F. Line a large baking sheet with parchment paper or a silicone baking mat; set aside.

2. To make the chocolate dough, place the chopped chocolate in the top half of a double boiler set over about 1 inch of simmering water. If you don't have a double boiler, place the chocolate in a medium bowl that fits snugly over a medium saucepan with a similar amount of simmering water. Stir until half the chocolate has melted, making sure none of the escaping steam gets into the chocolate and causes it to seize. Remove the top of the double boiler or the bowl from the heat and continue stirring until all the chocolate has melted. Cool for 5 minutes.

3. Meanwhile, continue making the chocolate dough by softening the butter in a large bowl with an electric mixer at medium speed, just until pale and somewhat airy, about 1 minute. Add the granulated sugar and continue beating until fluffy but still grainy, about 1 more minute. Beat in the egg and egg white, then the vanilla and salt until smooth. Turn off the mixer, add the flour, then beat at low speed just until a soft dough forms, about 20 seconds. Set this dough aside.

4. To prepare the peanut butter dough, clean and dry the beaters thoroughly. Soften the peanut butter and the butter in a second large bowl, using the electric mixer at medium speed, until fairly smooth, about 1 minute. Add the brown sugar and beat until light, about 2 more minutes. Beat in the egg yolk. Remove the beaters and stir in the flour and salt, using a wooden spoon or a rubber spatula, just until a creamy, smooth dough forms.

5. To make the cookies, roll a tablespoon of the chocolate dough into a ball, place it on the prepared baking sheet, and gently flatten it with your fingers into a 2-inch patty. Roll a teaspoon of the peanut butter dough into a ball, flatten it in the palm of your hand into a disk, and place it on top of the chocolate dough patty. Finally, roll ½ teaspoon of the chocolate dough into a ball, flatten as well, and place on top of the peanut butter patty, thereby creating the bull's-eye pattern. If desired, you can put a tiny dot of peanut butter dough right in the center of the pattern. Repeat, spacing each cookie about 2 inches apart.

6. Bake for 15 minutes, rotating the sheet back to front once during baking. The chocolate dough should feel set to the touch; the peanut butter will still be soft. Cool on the baking sheet for 3 minutes, then transfer the cookies to a wire rack to cool completely. Cool the baking sheet for 5 minutes before proceeding with another batch, or use a second lined baking sheet that hasn't been in the oven.

Mix It Up!

Chocolate Almond Bull's-eyes: Substitute 5 tablespoons almond butter for the peanut butter; add 1 tablespoon corn syrup with the brown sugar.

Chocolate Hazelnut Bull's-eyes: Decrease the butter in the peanut butter dough to 3 tablespoons; substitute 7 tablespoons Nutella or other hazelnut-chocolate spread for the peanut butter.

Chocolate Sesame Bull's-eyes: Substitute tahini for the peanut butter.

CHOCOLATE PEANUT BUTTER CREAM SANDWICHES

We made these classic cream sandwiches rectangular to look like little ice cream sandwiches. The cookies are crisp and chocolaty; the filling, rich and decadent. All in all, they're a terrific treat, whether for a back-to-school or end-of-school celebration. They're also wonderful right out of the freezer.

MAKES ABOUT 2 DOZEN LARGE SANDWICH COOKIES

FOR THE COOKIES

2¼	cups all-purpose flour
⅔	cup cocoa powder, preferably natural cocoa powder, sifted
½	teaspoon baking soda
½	teaspoon salt
12	tablespoons (1½ sticks) cool, unsalted butter, cut into small pieces
4	tablespoons solid vegetable shortening (2 ounces)
1⅓	cups granulated sugar
1	large egg, at room temperature
1	tablespoon vanilla extract

FOR THE FILLING

¾	cup creamy peanut butter
3	tablespoons unsalted butter, at room temperature
2	tablespoons light corn syrup
1	teaspoon vanilla extract
1	cup confectioners' sugar
2	tablespoons heavy cream

1. To make the cookies, whisk the flour, cocoa powder, baking soda, and salt in a medium bowl until uniform; set aside.

2. Using an electric mixer at medium speed, soften the butter and shortening in a large bowl until light and smooth, about 1 minute. Add the sugar and continue beating until fluffy but still grainy, about 1 more minute. Beat in the egg and vanilla until smooth. Remove the beaters and stir in the prepared flour mixture with a wooden spoon or a rubber spatula just until incorporated. The dough will be very soft but will hold together. Divide in half.

3. Sprinkle a few drops of water on your work surface, then lay a large sheet of plastic wrap on top. Place half the dough on it, then lay a second large sheet of plastic wrap over the dough, covering the bottom sheet. Roll the dough out to ¼ inch thick; gently transfer it, still between the sheets of plastic wrap, to a large ungreased baking sheet. Repeat this process with the other half of the dough. Refrigerate both baking sheets until the dough is firm, about 1 hour, but not more than 3 hours.

4. Position the rack in the center of the oven; preheat the oven to 350°F.

5. Once the dough is firm, remove one of the baking sheets from the refrigerator, slip the plastic-wrapped dough off it and onto your work surface, and peel off the top sheet of plastic wrap. Line the cold baking sheet with parchment paper or a silicone baking mat.

6. Working quickly, cut the cookies into 3 × 2-inch rectangles. Use a metal spatula to transfer these back to the baking sheet, spacing the rectangles about 2 inches apart. Prick them with a fork, to replicate the holes in a graham cracker.

7. Bake for about 13 minutes, rotating the sheet back to front once during baking. The cookies should be firm on top but a little spongy inside if touched. Cool for 2 minutes on the baking sheet, then transfer to a wire rack to cool completely. Repeat with the second half of the dough, rolling and baking as indicated, using the second cold baking sheet, lined with parchment paper or a silicone baking mat.

8. Once the cookies have cooled, make the filling by beating the peanut butter, butter, and corn syrup in a large bowl with an electric mixer at medium speed until very smooth and creamy, about 2 minutes. Beat in the vanilla, then add the confectioners' sugar in ¼-cup increments, beating each in thoroughly before adding the next. Scrape down the sides of the bowl as necessary. When all the confectioners' sugar has been added, continue beating until a thick, doughlike filling forms, about 2 minutes. Remove the beaters and stir in the cream until smooth and velvety.

9. Place 2 teaspoons of the peanut butter filling on the flat side of one of the rectangles; spread the filling evenly to the sides, using a small spatula, an offset spatula, or an icing knife. Top with a second cookie, flat side down. Place the filled cookie on a wire rack to allow the filling to firm, about 45 minutes. Continue making sandwich cookies until all the tops and bottoms are used.

Recommended storage
2 days at room temperature
3 months in the freezer

More Choices!

Chocolate Fluffernutter Cream Sandwiches: Make a half batch of the filling mixture. Spread 1 teaspoon Marshmallow Fluff on one cookie; spread 1 teaspoon peanut butter filling on another cookie; then sandwich these two cookies together, fillings inside. (You'll need about ½ cup Fluff.)

Chocolate Peanut Butter and Jam Cream Sandwiches: Make a half batch of the filling mixture. Spread 1 teaspoon grape jam on one cookie; spread 1 teaspoon filling on another cookie; then sandwich these two cookies together, fillings inside. (You'll need about ½ cup grape jelly.)

Chocolate Peanut Butter Crunchy Cream Sandwiches: Substitute crunchy peanut butter for the creamy peanut butter in the filling.

CHOCOLATE PEANUT BUTTER REFRIGERATOR COOKIES

Here's a light, crisp, and easy refrigerator cookie, one you can make in advance and bake as you need it. The chocolate flavor dominates, but if you let the dough sit in the refrigerator for at least 24 hours, the peanut butter taste will become more prominent.

MAKES ABOUT 3 DOZEN COOKIES

3	ounces unsweetened chocolate, chopped
2	cups all-purpose flour, plus additional for dusting
½	teaspoon baking soda
½	teaspoon salt
9	tablespoons (1 stick plus 1 tablespoon) cool, unsalted butter, cut into small pieces, plus additional for buttering the baking sheet
½	cup smooth peanut butter (do not use "natural" peanut butter)
1½	cups sugar
1	large egg, at room temperature
1	large egg white, at room temperature
1	teaspoon vanilla extract

1. Place the chocolate in the top half of a double boiler set over a little more than an inch of simmering water, or in a medium bowl that fits tightly over a medium pot with a similar amount of simmering water. Stir until half the chocolate has melted, taking care not to let any of the escaping steam get into the chocolate. Remove the top half of the double boiler or the bowl from the heat and continue stirring until the chocolate has completely melted. Cool for 5 minutes.

2. Whisk the flour, baking soda, and salt in a medium bowl until well combined; set aside. Cream the butter and peanut butter in a large bowl, using an electric mixer at medium speed, until light and smooth, about 1 minute. Add the sugar and beat at medium speed until light and pale brown, about 2 more minutes. Beat in the egg and egg white until fully incorporated, then the vanilla until smooth.

3. With the mixer running at low speed, beat in the melted chocolate by pouring it into the mixture in a slow, thin stream. Once the mixture is smooth and uniformly colored, remove the beaters and stir in the prepared flour mixture with a wooden spoon or a rubber spatula, just until the flour is moistened. The batter may be grainy, but no streaks of white should be visible.

4. Lightly flour a clean, dry work surface, then turn the dough out onto it. Knead it lightly for about 15 seconds, just until it adheres into a ball. Roll this ball into a log about 9 inches long and 2½ inches in diameter. Wrap tightly in plastic wrap and refrigerate for at least 4 hours or up to 3 days.

5. Position the rack in the center of the oven; preheat the oven to 350°F. Lightly butter a large baking sheet.

6. Unwrap the dough log and slice off disks ¼ inch thick. Space these disks 1 inch apart on the prepared baking sheet. Wrap any unused portion of the dough log in plastic wrap and store in the refrigerator until you're ready to bake additional batches.

7. Bake for about 10 minutes, rotating the sheet back to front halfway through baking, until the cookies are set but still soft to the touch, with very little browning. Cool on the baking sheet for 3 minutes, then transfer to a wire rack to cool completely. Cool the baking sheet for at least 5 minutes and lightly butter it a second time before baking a second batch.

Recommended storage
4 days at room temperature
3 months in the freezer after baking

Customize It!
Mix ⅔ cup of any of the following into the batter with the prepared flour mixture: chopped, unsalted macadamia nuts; chopped pecans; chopped walnuts, chopped, roasted, unsalted peanuts; dried currants; or mini chocolate chips.

CHOCOLATE PINWHEELS

These little round cookies pack an intense taste, thanks to interlocking swirls of chocolate and cream cheese. They're somewhat like refrigerator cookies: rolled and then sliced off a log as you bake them. Indeed, you could keep the logs tightly covered in the refrigerator for up to 3 days, slicing off and baking up cookies as you want them.

MAKES A LITTLE LESS THAN 4 DOZEN COOKIES

FOR THE CREAM CHEESE FILLING

4	ounces cream cheese (regular, low-fat, or nonfat), at room temperature
1/3	cup sugar
1	teaspoon all-purpose flour
1/2	teaspoon ground cinnamon
1	teaspoon vanilla extract
3/4	cup sliced almonds

FOR THE CHOCOLATE DOUGH

1 1/2	cups all-purpose flour
1/4	cup cocoa powder, sifted
1/2	teaspoon baking soda
1/4	teaspoon salt
6	tablespoons (3/4 stick) cool, unsalted butter, cut into small pieces
1	cup sugar
1	large egg, at room temperature

1. Make the cream cheese filling by beating the cream cheese and sugar in a medium bowl with an electric mixer at medium speed until light and airy, about 2 minutes. Scrape down the sides of the bowl and beat in the flour and cinnamon, then the vanilla, just until smooth, about 15 seconds. Stir in the sliced almonds with a wooden spoon or rubber spatula, then set the filling aside at room temperature.

2. To make the chocolate dough, whisk the flour, cocoa powder, baking soda, and salt in a medium bowl until uniform; set aside.

3. Clean and dry the electric beaters thoroughly, then soften the butter in a large bowl, using the mixer at medium speed, about 1 minute. Add the sugar and continue beating at medium speed until fluffy and pale yellow, if still grainy, about 1 more minute. Beat in the egg until well incorporated. Turn off the beaters, pour in the prepared flour mixture, and beat at a very low speed just until well mixed, about 30 seconds.

4. Sprinkle a few drops of water on your work surface, then lay out a large sheet of plastic wrap. (The water will help hold the plastic wrap in place.) Gather the dough into a ball and place it in the center of the plastic wrap. Flatten the dough slightly, then cover with a second large sheet of plastic wrap. Roll into a 9 × 16-inch rectangle, rearranging the top sheet of plastic wrap if it bunches up. Peel off the top sheet, then spread the cream cheese filling across the chocolate dough, using an offset spatula or a rubber spatula dipped in a little water. Leave a 1-inch border around all the edges of the chocolate dough.

5. Beginning with one of the long ends of the rectangle, roll the dough up jelly-roll style, using the bottom layer of plastic wrap to help you lift and roll the dough onto itself, but taking care not to get the plastic wrap caught up in the log. Roll tightly but don't press down—the idea is to have no air pockets—in other words, don't let the filling mush out the ends. Wrap the log in a new sheet of plastic wrap and refrigerate for at least 4 hours or up to 3 days. You can also freeze the log for up to 1 month; let it thaw in the refrigerator for 2 hours.

6. Position the rack in the center of the oven. Preheat the oven to 350°F. Line a large baking sheet with parchment paper or a silicone baking mat; set aside.

7. Unwrap the log and slice off cookies a little less than ½ inch thick, spacing them about 1½ inches apart on the baking sheet. Rewrap any unused dough and return it to the refrigerator. The ends of the log have little to no filling—either bake them as plain cookies or discard them.

8. Bake for about 12 minutes, rotating the sheet front to back halfway through baking, until the cookies are firm and set but the tops are slightly soft. Cool on the baking sheet for 2 minutes, then use a metal spatula to transfer the cookies to a wire rack to cool completely. Cool the baking sheet for 5 minutes before baking additional batches; if using parchment paper, replace it if it's crackly, browned, or torn.

> **Recommended storage**
> *4 days at room temperature*
> *2 months in the freezer after baking*

Personalize It!

Chocolate Apple Pinwheels: Reduce the almonds to ¼ cup; add ½ cup finely chopped dried apples with the remaining almonds.

Chocolate Coconut Pinwheels: Substitute unsweetened coconut chips for the almonds.

Chocolate Currant Pinwheels: Reduce the almonds to ¼ cup; add ½ cup dried currants with the remaining almonds.

Chocolate Pecan Pinwheels: Substitute finely chopped pecans for the almonds.

CHOCOLATE PRETZELS

You'll fake out your friends with these dark, chocolaty pretzel-shaped cookies. They look amazingly like the real thing—especially if you use clear coarse sugar, which looks like salt crystals. We've given these to friends who claim they taste the salt on the outside! No way—it's pure chocolate bliss all the way through.

MAKES ABOUT 18 COOKIES

1	ounce unsweetened chocolate, chopped
2	cups all-purpose flour
¼	cup cocoa powder, preferably natural, sifted
¼	teaspoon salt
10	tablespoons (1 stick plus 2 tablespoons) cool, unsalted butter, cut into small pieces
⅔	cup granulated sugar
1	large egg, at room temperature
½	teaspoon vanilla extract
1	large egg white, whisked with 1 tablespoon water in a small bowl until foamy
½	cup clear sanding sugar or clear coarse sugar (see page 20)

1. Place the chocolate in a small bowl and microwave on high for 15 seconds. Stir, then continue heating and stirring in 15-second increments until half the chocolate has melted. Remove the bowl from the microwave oven and continue stirring until all the chocolate has melted. Alternatively, place the chocolate in the top half of a double boiler set over about 1 inch of simmering water; stir until half the chocolate has melted, then remove the double boiler's top half from the heat and continue stirring until all the chocolate has melted. Set aside to cool for 5 minutes.

2. Whisk the flour, cocoa powder, and salt in a medium bowl until uniformly colored; set aside.

3. Soften the butter in a large bowl, using an electric mixer at medium speed, about 1 minute. Add the sugar and beat until light and airy, about 1 more minute. Beat in the egg, then the vanilla until smooth. Scrape down the sides of the bowl, then beat in the melted chocolate, pouring it into the bowl in a thin, steady stream with the beaters running. Turn off the beaters, pour in the prepared flour mixture, and beat at a very low speed just until a somewhat soft, pliable, but not smooth dough forms. Gather the dough into a ball while it's still in the bowl, then cover with a clean kitchen towel and set aside at room temperature for 30 minutes so that the glutens begin to set up.

4. Meanwhile, position the racks in the top and bottom thirds of the oven; preheat the oven to 375°F. Line two large baking sheets with parchment paper or a silicone baking mat; set aside.

5. Scoop out 2 tablespoons of the dough and roll it out into a 10-inch rope on a clean, dry work surface. Dust with flour if necessary. With the rope in front of you horizontally, curve the left end up and over a point about a third of the way in from the right end, then curve the right end up and over a point about a third of the way from the original left end—in other words, creating a pretzel. Place on the prepared sheet and brush lightly with the egg-white wash. Sprinkle liberally with the sanding or coarse sugar. Repeat with the remaining dough, making more pretzels and spacing them 2 inches apart on the baking sheets.

6. Bake for 7 minutes, then reverse the sheets back to front and top to bottom. Continue baking for about 7 more minutes, or until the cookies are set but somewhat springy to the touch. Cool on the baking sheets for 2 minutes, then transfer to wire racks to cool completely. Cool the baking sheets for 5 minutes before baking additional batches, if necessary.

Recommended storage
4 days at room temperature
2 months in the freezer

CHOCOLATE RAVIOLI COOKIES

These cookies are like round ravioli: tender, buttery cookie shells encasing a classic ganache filling, that divine mixture of chocolate and cream. If you use a fluted, round cookie cutter, they'll look even more like their namesakes. The cookies are quite delicate, so store them in a single layer—if there are any left to store!

MAKES ABOUT 2 DOZEN STUFFED COOKIES

FOR THE COOKIES

8	tablespoons (1 stick) unsalted butter, at room temperature
¼	cup solid vegetable shortening (2 ounces)
½	cup confectioners' sugar
¼	cup packed light brown sugar
2	large egg yolks, at room temperature
1	teaspoon vanilla extract
1¾	cups all-purpose flour, plus additional for dusting
⅛	teaspoon salt

FOR THE GANACHE FILLING

4	ounces semisweet chocolate, chopped (do not use bittersweet chocolate)
⅓	cup heavy cream

1. Soften the butter and shortening in a large bowl, using an electric mixer at medium speed, until light and somewhat smooth, about 1 minute. Add the confectioners' sugar and brown sugar and continue beating until pale yellow and light, if a little grainy, about 2 more minutes. Beat in the egg yolks one at a time, then the vanilla just until evenly colored. Turn off the beaters, add the flour and salt, then beat at a very low speed just until a soft, wet dough forms. Divide the dough in half, wrap each in plastic wrap, flatten slightly into thick disks, and refrigerate for 2 hours, or until the dough is firm enough to roll out.

2. Fifteen minutes before rolling out the cookies, prepare the ganache filling. Place the chocolate in a medium bowl. Heat the cream in a small saucepan over low heat until barely simmering. Pour the cream over the chocolate and stir with a wooden spoon until the chocolate has melted. Set aside at room temperature while the dough continues to chill.

3. Position the rack in the top third of the oven; preheat the oven to 350°F.

4. Lightly dust a clean, dry work surface with flour and place one of the pieces of dough on it. Dust the dough and a rolling pin lightly with flour. Roll out to a very thin sheet, only ⅛ inch thick. Use a 2½-inch, round cookie cutter, lightly dusted with flour, to cut out disks. Separate the disks from the dough sheet. (You may gather any scraps together, refrigerate them again, and reroll them, although the additional flour from dusting will have toughened the dough considerably.)

5. Place 1 teaspoon of the ganache filling in the center of half of the cut-out disks. Cover each with a second disk, then gently pinch the edges together all around to seal the disks closed and create a little pocket cookie. Two warnings: (1) the dough is very fragile, so work quickly and efficiently; and (2) the edges must be completely sealed before baking. If desired, crimp the edges into a decorative pattern.

6. Place the pillows on a large, ungreased baking sheet, preferably nonstick, spacing them about 1½ inches apart. If all the pillows don't fit on one sheet, cover the remainder with a clean, dry kitchen towel—or bake the first batch while preparing a second on a second baking sheet.

7. Bake for about 16 minutes, or until lightly browned at the edges. The tops of the pillows will be rounded and somewhat firm to the touch. Use a metal spatula to transfer the cookies immediately to a wire rack, thereby preventing the bottoms from browning further. Cool the baking sheet for 10 minutes before proceeding with the remaining dough, using the rest of the refrigerated dough to make more pockets.

> **Recommended storage**
> *3 days at room temperature*
> *Not recommended for freezing*

Customize It!

Before baking, you can brush the cookies lightly with a mixture of 1 large egg white beaten in a small bowl with 2 teaspoons water until foamy. Then sprinkle the cookies with any of the following (you'll need about ½ cup total volume): finely chopped pecans, shredded coconut, or sliced almonds.

Or mix 2 tablespoons superfine sugar and 2 teaspoons ground cinnamon in a small bowl. Brush the cookies with the egg-white wash as above, then dust them with the cinnamon sugar before baking.

Or forgo the egg-white wash, bake the cookies as directed, then when they're completely cooled, dust them with a mixture of 3 tablespoons confectioners' sugar and 1 tablespoon cocoa powder.

CHOCOLATE REFRIGERATOR COOKIES

This is the simplest way to get a chocolate-cookie fix! You can make the dough in advance and store it in the refrigerator for up to 1 week, baking as many or as few of these buttery cookies as you want—or need.

MAKES ABOUT 4 DOZEN COOKIES

2⅓ cups all-purpose flour, plus additional for dusting
½ cup cocoa powder, sifted
¼ teaspoon salt
½ pound (2 sticks) cool, unsalted butter, cut into small pieces
1 cup sugar
2 large egg yolks, at room temperature
1 teaspoon vanilla extract

1. Whisk the flour, cocoa powder, and salt in a medium bowl until uniformly colored. Set aside.

2. Soften the butter in a large bowl, using an electric mixer at medium speed, about 2 minutes. Add the sugar and continue beating until light and pale yellow, but still a little grainy, about 2 more minutes. Add the egg yolks one at a time, beating in the first before adding the second. Beat in the vanilla.

3. Remove the beaters and stir in the prepared flour mixture with a wooden spoon or a rubber spatula, just until the flour is moistened and the dough begins to turn into grainy threads.

4. Lightly dust a clean, dry work surface with flour, turn the dough onto it, and gather into a uniform ball. Shape into a log about 12 inches long and 1½ inches in diameter. Seal in plastic wrap and refrigerate until firm, at least 4 hours or up to 1 week.

5. To bake the cookies, position the racks in the top and bottom thirds of the oven; preheat the oven to 350°F. Unwrap the log and slice it into ¼-inch-thick disks. Place these on two ungreased baking sheets, preferably nonstick, spacing the disks about 1 inch apart. Rewrap and refrigerate the remaining dough log until needed, either after the cookies have baked or for another day entirely. You can also freeze the remaining log, wrapped tightly in plastic wrap, for up to 3 months; thaw in the refrigerator for 2 hours before slicing into cookies.

6. Bake for about 8 minutes, then rotate the sheets top to bottom and front to back. Bake for about 7 more minutes, or until the cookies are set and firm to the touch although just a little soft inside. Cool for 1 minute on the baking sheets, then transfer to wire racks to cool completely. Cool the baking sheets for at least 5 minutes before baking more cookies.

Recommended storage
2 days at room temperature
Once baked, 1 month in the freezer

More Choices!

Chocolate Almond Refrigerator Cookies: Substitute almond extract for the vanilla extract; stir ⅓ cup sliced almonds into the batter with the flour mixture.

Chocolate Cashew Refrigerator Cookies: Add: ⅓ cup finely chopped unsalted roasted cashews with the flour mixture.

Chocolate Coconut Refrigerator Cookies: Add ⅓ cup sweetened shredded coconut with the flour mixture.

Chocolate Date Spiced Refrigerator Cookies: Stir ½ teaspoon ground ginger and ¼ teaspoon ground allspice into the dry ingredients with the flour; stir in ⅓ cup chopped pitted dates with the vanilla extract.

Chocolate Maple Refrigerator Cookies: Reduce sugar to ⅔ cup; add ⅓ cup maple sugar with the remaining sugar. Substitute maple flavoring for the vanilla extract.

Chocolate Spiced Refrigerator Cookies: Stir ¾ teaspoon ground ginger, ½ teaspoon ground cinnamon, ¼ teaspoon ground cloves, and ¼ teaspoon grated nutmeg into the dry ingredients with the flour.

CHOCOLATE RUGELACH

Part pastry and part cookie, our rugelach are somewhat less sweet than those found in bake shops. We like the combination of whole wheat pastry flour and all-purpose flour because it gives the treats a hearty, slightly nutty taste. If you can't find whole wheat pastry flour (available in many gourmet markets and from outlets liked in the Source Guide, page 229), substitute white cake flour.

MAKES ABOUT 32 RUGELACH

1½	cups whole wheat pastry flour
1	cup all-purpose flour
½	teaspoon salt
½	pound (2 sticks) cool, unsalted butter, cut into small pieces, plus additional for greasing the baking sheets
8	ounces cream cheese (regular or low-fat, but not nonfat), softened
3	tablespoons sugar
1	large egg, at room temperature
1	teaspoon vanilla extract
8	ounces semisweet or bittersweet chocolate, chopped
1	cup finely chopped walnuts

1. Mix the whole wheat pastry flour, all-purpose flour, and salt in a medium bowl until well combined. Set aside.

2. Use an electric mixer at medium speed to soften and blend the butter and cream cheese in a large bowl, about 1 minute. Add the sugar and beat the mixture until soft and quite light, about 2 more minutes. Beat in the egg and vanilla until smooth.

3. Remove the beaters and stir in the flour mixture with a wooden spoon just until a soft dough forms. Gather the dough into a ball without kneading. Wrap in plastic wrap and refrigerate until chilled, at least 4 hours or up to 24 hours.

4. Position the rack in the middle of the oven; preheat the oven to 400°F. Lightly butter two large baking sheets and set them aside.

5. Place the chocolate in the top half of a double boiler set over a little more than 1 inch of simmering water. If you don't have a double boiler, use a medium bowl that fits snugly over a medium saucepan with a similar amount of simmering water. Take care that no steam gets into the melting chocolate; adjust the heat to maintain a gentle simmer, not a rolling boil. Stir until half the chocolate has melted, then remove the double boiler's top half or the bowl from the simmering water and continue stirring until all the chocolate has melted. Set aside to cool for 5 minutes.

6. Divide the chilled dough in half. Lightly dust a clean, dry work surface and a rolling pin with flour. Place half the dough on the work surface, then roll it into a circle about 12 inches in diameter and a little less than ¼ inch thick. Spread this circle with half the melted chocolate, leaving a 1-inch border around the circumference. Sprinkle the chocolate coating with half the chopped nuts.

7. Work quickly so you can finish making the rugelach before the chocolate hardens. Use a pizza roller or a long, sharp knife to cut the circle into 16 wedges, like cutting a pizza into 16 slices. Separate these slices from the whole, then, starting at the wide edge, roll each one up toward the point of the wedge. Place them, tip side down, on one of the prepared baking sheets, spacing them 1 inch apart.

8. Bake for 12 to 15 minutes until lightly browned and firm to the touch. Cool for 2 minutes on the baking sheet, then transfer them to a wire rack to cool completely.

9. Prepare the second half of the dough, rolling it out, coating it in chocolate and nuts, cutting it into slices, rolling the slices up—just as you did with the first half. Place these on the second prepared baking sheet and bake as indicated.

Recommended storage
3 days at room temperature
2 months in the freezer

Customize It!
Substitute chopped hazelnuts or chopped pecans for the walnuts. Or reduce the walnuts to ½ cup and add ½ cup chopped apricots, chopped dates, chopped figs, raisins, or sweetened shredded coconut with the remaining nuts.

CHOCOLATE SANDIES

The addition of chocolate makes these a little moister—and certainly even better—than traditional pecan sandies. Allow the cookies to cool completely before serving so they'll still have that delicious crack.

MAKES ABOUT 3½ DOZEN COOKIES

5	cups pecan pieces
⅔	cup granulated sugar
1½	cups all-purpose flour
⅓	cup cocoa powder, preferably Dutch-processed, sifted
½	teaspoon baking soda
¼	teaspoon salt
1	cup packed light brown sugar
½	cup solid vegetable shortening (4 ounces), plus additional for greasing the baking sheets
1	large egg, at room temperature
1	teaspoon vanilla extract
2	large egg whites, beaten in a small bowl with 2 tablespoons water until foamy

1. Position the racks in the top and bottom thirds of the oven; preheat the oven to 350°F. Use a small dab of shortening on a piece of crumpled wax paper to grease two large baking sheets; set aside.

2. First, prepare the various dry ingredients needed for the recipe. Place 2 cups of the pecans in a food processor fitted with a chopping blade; process until the texture of finely ground meal but not pastelike; set aside in a small bowl. Place the remaining 3 cups pecans and all the granulated sugar in the food processor; process until sandy, pour onto a large plate, and set aside. Finally, whisk the flour, cocoa powder, baking soda, and salt in a medium bowl until evenly colored; set aside as well.

3. Using an electric mixer at medium speed, beat the brown sugar and shortening in a large bowl, until smooth and creamy, about 2 minutes. Beat in the whole egg, then the vanilla, until smooth. Pour in the ground pecans (the ones *without* the sugar) and beat for about 10 seconds just until incorporated. Remove the beaters and stir in the prepared flour mixture with a wooden spoon or a spatula until a thick dough forms. Set aside for 10 minutes to firm a bit.

4. Pinch off a piece of dough about the size of a walnut and roll between your hands into a 1-inch ball. Dip this ball in the egg-white mixture; then roll into the pecan and sugar mixture, coating the ball completely. Place on one of the prepared baking sheets, then continue making pecan-coated balls, spacing them about 2 inches apart. Reserve any unused dough for a second round of baking.

5. Bake for 12 minutes, then rotate the sheets front to back and top to bottom. At this time, flatten the cookies slightly with a heat-safe rubber spatula or the back of a flatware spoon, just to remove their rounded tops. Continue baking for 5 to 6 more minutes, or until the cookies are lightly browned and cracked at the edges. Cool on the baking sheets for 2 minutes, then transfer to wire racks to cool completely. Cool the baking sheets for 5 more minutes, then lightly grease them again before making additional batches, if necessary.

Recommended storage
3 days at room temperature
2 months in the freezer

Personalize It!
Mix in ½ cup of any of the following with the ground pecans: chopped dried mango, chopped pitted dates, dried currants, golden raisins, M&M's Mini Baking Bits, Reese's Pieces, unsweetened coconut chips, or white chocolate chips.

And/or spice the batter with one of the following, added with the ground pecans: 2 teaspoons apple pie spice mix, 1 teaspoon ground cinnamon, 1 teaspoon ground ginger, ½ teaspoon grated nutmeg, or ¼ teaspoon cayenne.

CHOCOLATE SHORTBREAD

We modeled these cookies on those popular, store-bought shortbread rounds divided into pie-shaped wedges. These are made with unsweetened chocolate for a deep, sophisticated taste.

MAKES ABOUT 18 LARGE SHORTBREAD ROUNDS

3	ounces unsweetened chocolate, chopped
½	pound (2 sticks) cool, unsalted butter, cut into small pieces
1	cup confectioners' sugar
1	teaspoon vanilla extract
1½	cups all-purpose flour
½	teaspoon salt

1. Place the chocolate in the top half of a double boiler set over about 1 inch of simmering water, or place it in a medium bowl that fits over a medium saucepan with about the same amount of simmering water. Stir until half the chocolate has melted, then remove the top half of the double boiler or the bowl from the heat and continue stirring until all the chocolate has melted. Set aside to cool for 5 minutes.

2. Soften the butter in a large bowl, using an electric mixer at medium speed, about 2 minutes. Add the confectioners' sugar and beat the mixture at medium speed until smooth, about 1 more minute. Beat in the vanilla, then the cooled, melted chocolate until uniform. Remove the beaters and stir in the flour and salt with a wooden spoon or a rubber spatula, just until moistened and incorporated but not sticky. The dough should be soft but hold together. Let stand for 5 minutes.

3. Sprinkle a few drops of water on your work surface, then lay a large sheet of plastic wrap on top. Turn the chocolate dough out onto the plastic wrap; flatten into a thick, round disk; then cover with a second large sheet of plastic wrap. Roll to a circle about ½ inch thick, or thinner for crisper cookies, but no thinner than

⅓ inch. Using the plastic wrap, transfer the circle of dough to a baking sheet and refrigerate until firm and cold, about 1 hour, but not more than 2 hours.

4. Position the rack in the center of the oven; preheat the oven to 350°F. Line a second large baking sheet with parchment paper or a silicone baking mat; set aside.

5. Remove the circle of dough from the refrigerator, then transfer it from the baking sheet to your work surface. Remove the top sheet of plastic wrap and cut the dough into large, circular cookies, using a 3-inch cookie cutter or a drinking glass with a similarly sized rim. Transfer these rounds to the prepared baking sheet, spacing them 1 inch apart. Use the back of a flatware knife to score each of these rounds into 6 pie-wedge sections. Do not cut through. You can also make small, dotlike indentations in the sections with the tip of the knife if you like—but again do not poke through to the baking sheet. If all the cookies will not fit on one baking sheet, line another with parchment paper or a silicone baking mat, transfer these cookies to it, then place it in the refrigerator until the first batch has baked; let stand at room temperature for 3 minutes before placing it in the oven.

6. Bake for 6 minutes, reverse the sheet from back to front, and continue baking for about 6 more minutes, or until the rounds are dry but soft. The tops should have tiny, raised air pockets, somewhat like goose bumps. The cookies should give a bit when touched—do not overbake. Cool on the baking sheet for 5 minutes, then transfer the cookies to a wire rack to cool completely.

Recommended storage
3 days at room temperature
2 months in the freezer

Personalize It!

Once you roll out the dough, you can cut it into any number of shapes. Smaller shapes require a shorter baking time—2-inch hearts, for example, bake for about 10 minutes.

Once the cookies are cooled, you can ice them with a thin layer of either the chocolate or vanilla icing found with the Black Black and Whites (page 33)—or you can make both and frost half the cookies in chocolate and half in vanilla, spreading on a thin layer with an offset spatula.

CHOCOLATE SNICKERDOODLES

Ah, snickerdoodles, a childhood pleasure: rolled in cinnamon and sugar, moist but crackly. We've rolled this chocolate version in that traditional sugary mix—when combined with the chocolate in the cookies, it gives them a taste somewhat reminiscent of spicy Mexican chocolate cookies.

MAKES A LITTLE MORE THAN 3 DOZEN COOKIES

2	cups all-purpose flour
½	cup cocoa powder, preferably natural, sifted
½	teaspoon baking soda
¼	teaspoon salt
1⅔	cups plus ¼ cup sugar
1	tablespoon ground cinnamon
¾	cup solid vegetable shortening (6 ounces)
2	large eggs, at room temperature
1	teaspoon vanilla extract

1. Position the rack in the center of the oven; preheat the oven to 350°F. Use a small dab of shortening on a piece of crumpled wax paper to grease a large baking sheet.

2. Mix the flour, cocoa powder, baking soda, and salt in a medium bowl until uniform; set aside. Mix ¼ cup of the sugar with the cinnamon in a small, wide-mouthed bowl or teacup; set aside as well.

3. Cream the remaining 1⅔ cups sugar and the shortening in a large bowl, using an electric mixer at medium speed, until soft and light, about 2 minutes. Scrape down the sides of the bowl, then beat in the eggs one at a time, making sure the first is completely incorporated before adding the second. Beat in the vanilla. Turn off the mixer, add the prepared flour mixture, then beat at low speed just until the dough adheres into crumbly bits. Do not beat until it gathers into a ball; instead, remove the mixer, clean and dry your hands, then use them to finish off the dough, mixing a little more and bringing it together as a large although grainy ball.

4. Pinch off a piece of dough about the size of a walnut; roll into a 1-inch ball between your palms. Roll this ball into the sugar and cinnamon mixture. Place it on the prepared baking sheet. Continue making these coated balls, spacing them about 1½ inches apart on the sheet.

5. Bake for 14 minutes, then give the baking sheet a hard rap against the oven rack and bake for about 2 more minutes, or until the cookies are slightly cracked at the edges and feel dry but still soft to the touch. Cool for 2 minutes on the baking sheet, then transfer to a wire rack to cool completely. Cool the baking sheet for 5 minutes before greasing it again and baking additional batches.

> **Recommended storage**
> *3 days at room temperature*
> *3 months in the freezer*

Mix It Up!
Mix ⅔ cup of any of the following into the batter with the flour mixture: chopped chocolate-covered espresso beans, chopped hazelnuts, chopped pitted dates, chopped walnuts, cocoa nibs, golden raisins, M&M's Mini Baking Bits, mini chocolate chips, Reese's Pieces, or salted peanuts (if used, omit the salt in the dry ingredients).

CHOCOLATE SPRITZ COOKIES

Spritz cookies are a Scandinavian specialty: pressed cookies in all sorts of shapes. The chocolate dough in this recipe is quite soft, but don't refrigerate it. It's best to simply let it stand at room temperature for 5 minutes before pressing out the cookies. You'll need a cookie press, found at many specialty kitchenware stores or from outlets listed in the Source Guide (page 229).

MAKES ABOUT 8 DOZEN TINY COOKIES

2	cups all-purpose flour
6	tablespoons cocoa powder, sifted
½	teaspoon salt
1	ounce unsweetened chocolate, chopped
½	pound (2 sticks) cool, unsalted butter, cut into small pieces
⅔	cup sugar
1	large egg yolk, at room temperature
1	teaspoon vanilla extract
1	large egg white, beaten in a small bowl with 2 tablespoons water until frothy
½	cup sanding sugar, of any color or colors (see page 20)

1. Position the racks in the top and bottom thirds of the oven; preheat the oven to 350°F. Line two large baking sheets with silicone baking mats or parchment paper; set aside. Whisk the flour, cocoa, and salt in a medium bowl until well combined; set aside as well.

2. Place the chocolate in a small bowl and microwave on high in 15-second increments, stirring after each, until half the chocolate has melted. Remove the bowl from the microwave oven and continue stirring until all the chocolate has melted. Alternatively, place the chocolate in the top half of a double boiler set over about 1 inch of simmering water; stir until half the chocolate has melted, then remove the double boiler's top half from the heat and continue stirring until all the chocolate has melted. In any case, cool the melted chocolate for 5 minutes before proceeding.

3. Use an electric mixer at medium speed to soften the butter in a large bowl, about 1 minute. Add the sugar and continue beating at medium speed until light and fluffy, about 1 more minute. Beat in the egg yolk, then the cooled, melted chocolate and the vanilla until smooth. Turn off the beaters, add the prepared flour mixture, and beat at low speed just until a soft, pliable dough forms. Let rest for 5 minutes.

4. Gather as much of the dough as will fill the cookie press tube, seal it with the plunger and cutting design of your choice, then press out the cookies onto the prepared baking sheets as indicated by the manufacturer's instructions. Lightly brush the cookies with the egg-white mixture, then sprinkle a small amount of sanding sugar over each.

5. Bake for 7 minutes, then reverse the sheets back to front and top to bottom. Continue baking for about 6 minutes, or until the cookies are set but still a little soft to the touch. Do not let them brown. Cool on the baking sheets for 1 minute, then transfer to wire racks to cool completely. Cool the baking sheets for 5 minutes before baking additional batches.

Recommended storage
1 week at room temperature
3 months in the freezer

Tips for Spritz Success
The raw cookies can only stick to cool baking sheets. For best results, place the sheets in the refrigerator for 5 minutes to cool them down before pressing the cookies onto them.

Don't be hesitant: Squeeze the cookie onto the sheet and release with a quick jerk.

Don't cool the cookies for more than 1 minute on the baking sheets; the melted sugar will glue them down.

CHOCOLATE SUGAR COOKIES

These are some of the best sugar cookies we've eaten: moist yet crisp, tender yet sturdy enough to dunk—and best of all, loaded with chocolate! Grating the chocolate keeps the cocoa butter from melting into the batter and causing the cookies to spread. Our secret for getting the sugar coating to stick to the cookies? Use a drinking glass to press the crystals into the cookies as you flatten them.

MAKES ABOUT 3½ DOZEN COOKIES

2	cups all-purpose flour, plus additional for dusting
¼	cup cocoa powder, preferably natural, sifted
4	ounces semisweet chocolate, grated (see Chocolate Grater, page 15)
6	tablespoons cool, unsalted butter, cut into small pieces
5	tablespoons solid vegetable shortening (2½ ounces)
¾	cup granulated sugar
1	large egg, at room temperature
1½	tablespoons milk (regular, low-fat, or nonfat)
1	teaspoon vanilla extract
½	cup sanding sugar or coarse sugar, preferably clear (see page 20), spread on a plate

1. Position the racks in the top and bottom thirds of the oven; preheat the oven to 375°F. Whisk the flour, cocoa powder, and grated chocolate in a medium bowl until uniform; set aside.

2. Place the butter and shortening in a large bowl and use an electric mixer at medium speed to soften them into a fairly smooth mass. Add the sugar and beat until fluffy but still a little grainy, about 1 more minute. Beat in the egg until smooth, then beat in the milk and vanilla. Stop the beaters, add the flour mixture, then beat at low speed just until a dry, rough dough forms.

3. Dust a clean, dry work surface with the smallest sprinkling of flour, then turn the dough out onto it and knead for a few turns, just until it coheres into a fairly smooth ball. Break off walnut-size pieces, roll them into balls between your palms, and place them 2 inches apart on two large nonstick baking sheets.

4. Press the bottom of a medium drinking glass into the remaining, unused dough, then press the glass's bottom into the sanding or coarse sugar (the grease from the dough will help the crystals adhere to the glass). Use the bottom of the glass to flatten the cookies gently, pressing down to let the crystals adhere, until the cookies are about ½ inch thick. Repeat until all the balls are flattened and coated in sugar.

5. Bake for 5 minutes, then reverse the sheets top to bottom and front to back. Continue baking for about 5 more minutes, or until the cookies are dry at the edges and somewhat firm to the touch. Cool on the sheet for 1 minute, then transfer to wire racks to cool completely. Cool the baking sheets for 5 minutes before baking additional batches. When you run out of dough to press the glass into, you can lightly spray the glass with nonstick spray, but it should be well greased by this point and need no additional help to get the sugar to adhere.

Recommended storage
4 days at room temperature
3 months in the freezer

More Choices!

Chocolate Cinnamon Sugar Cookies: Substitute granulated sugar for the sanding or coarse sugar; mix 1 tablespoon ground cinnamon into the granulated sugar before coating the cookies.

Chocolate Nib Cookies: Substitute cocoa nibs for the sanding or coarse sugar.

White Chocolate Almond Sugar Cookies: Substitute grated white chocolate for the semisweet chocolate; substitute almond extract for the vanilla extract.

White Chocolate Banana Sugar Cookies: Substitute grated white chocolate for the semisweet chocolate; substitute banana flavoring for the vanilla extract.

White Chocolate Sugar Cookies: Substitute grated white chocolate for the semisweet chocolate.

CHOCOLATE TEA COOKIES

These cookies are not particularly sweet, but the cocoa powder keeps them from being too dry or crackly. While they are excellent with a cup of tea (or coffee), we suggest pairing them with a scoop of mango sorbet on a summer afternoon—or any afternoon that could use a bit of summer.

MAKES ABOUT 4½ DOZEN COOKIES

2½ cups all-purpose flour
½ cup cocoa powder, preferably Dutch-processed, sifted
2 teaspoons baking powder
½ teaspoon salt
1 cup sugar
¼ cup solid vegetable shortening (2 ounces)
⅔ cup canola or vegetable oil
2 large eggs, at room temperature
1 teaspoon vanilla extract

1. Position the oven racks in the top and bottom thirds of the oven. Preheat the oven to 350°F. Whisk the flour, cocoa powder, baking powder, and salt in a medium bowl until well combined, without streaks of white flour; set aside.

2. Beat the sugar and shortening in a large bowl with an electric mixer at medium speed until soft and frosting-like, if still a little grainy, about 2 minutes. With the beaters running, slowly drizzle in the oil, scraping down the sides of the bowl as necessary; continue beating until smooth. Beat in the eggs and vanilla. Turn off the mixer, add the flour, and beat at low speed just until a soft dough forms, a little less than 1 minute.

3. Once a soft dough forms, remove the beaters and scrape any dough that adheres to the beaters back into the bowl. Roll the dough into 1-inch balls and place them about 1½ inches apart on two large, nonstick, ungreased baking sheets. Roll only as many balls as will fit on the sheets for each baking—keep the remaining dough in the bowl and cover the bowl with a clean kitchen towel. Use a fork to press the balls into a cross-hatch pattern, first pressing in one direction, then rotating the tines 90 degrees and pressing again. Don't smash the dough balls flat; just press down with a firm but still delicate pressure.

4. Bake for 12 minutes, switching the sheets on the racks halfway through and rotating them 90 degrees. When baked, the cookies should feel dry and should have firm cracks around the edges. Cool on the sheets for 2 minutes, then transfer the cookies to a wire rack to cool completely. Let the baking sheets cool for 5 minutes before proceeding with additional batches.

Recommended storage
1 week at room temperature
3 months in the freezer

Customize It!
Substitute any of the following for the vanilla extract: 1 teaspoon coconut flavoring, 1 teaspoon maple flavoring, 1 teaspoon orange extract, 1 teaspoon raspberry flavoring, 1 teaspoon rum extract, ½ teaspoon almond extract, or ½ teaspoon mint extract.

CHOCOLATE TRUFFLE SANDWICH COOKIES

These tender chocolate cookies surround a luscious filling reminiscent of dark chocolate truffles. The cookies are so rich, they almost melt in your mouth. Make sure you have plenty of friends on hand to share them.

MAKES ABOUT 1½ DOZEN COOKIES

FOR THE COOKIES

½	cup walnut pieces
1	cup all-purpose flour
⅓	cup cocoa powder, sifted
¼	cup cornstarch
⅛	teaspoon salt
18	tablespoons (2 sticks plus 2 tablespoons) cool, unsalted butter, cut into small pieces
1¼	cups confectioners' sugar
½	teaspoon vanilla

FOR THE TRUFFLE FILLING

5	ounces bittersweet chocolate, chopped
¼	cup heavy cream
1½	tablespoons unsalted butter, at room temperature

1. To make the cookies, position the rack in the center of the oven and preheat the oven to 350°F. Place the walnuts on a large baking sheet and toast until lightly browned, stirring often, about 8 minutes. Cool the nuts completely, then grind them to a fine powder in a food processor fitted with the chopping blade. Pour the ground nuts into a medium bowl and whisk in the flour, cocoa powder, cornstarch, and salt until well combined; set aside.

2. Using an electric mixer at medium speed soften the butter in a large bowl for a little more than 1 minute. Add the confectioners' sugar and continue beating until light and icing-like, about 2 minutes. Beat in the vanilla, then slowly beat in the prepared flour mixture at low speed, adding the mixture in ½-cup increments; continue beating just until a very soft dough forms. Cover the bowl with plastic wrap and refrigerate until firm, about 2 hours.

3. Roll tablespoonfuls of the dough into 1-inch balls and place these about 2 inches apart on a large, nonstick, ungreased baking sheet. Refrigerate any remaining dough for a second baking.

4. Bake about 15 minutes, or until flattened, crackly, and set, but still somewhat soft. Cool on the baking sheet for 3 minutes, then use a metal spatula to transfer the cookies gently to a wire rack to cool completely. Cool the baking sheet for at least 5 minutes before using it again. Repeat the baking process until all the dough is used, thereby making about 36 big soft cookies.

5. When the cookies have cooled, place the chocolate in a medium bowl. Heat the cream over medium-low heat in a small saucepan until bubbles form around the edges, about 2 minutes. Pour the warmed cream over the chocolate and stir until all the chocolate has melted and the mixture is smooth. Add the butter and beat with an electric mixer at low speed until cooled and slightly thickened. Do not overbeat or the chocolate will seize—beat only until the color just begins to lighten slightly (see Note).

6. Spread 2 tablespoons of this mixture on the flat bottom of one of the cookies; sandwich it with the bottom of a second cookie. Continue until you have made about 18 chocolate sandwiches.

NOTE: *If the chocolate firms up too much as you fill the sandwiches, all is not lost. Simply roll about 2 tablespoons of the filling between your palms, like a chocolate truffle, then flatten it out with your fingers and sandwich this disk between 2 cookies, as indicated in the recipe.*

Recommended storage
3 days at room temperature
Not recommended for freezing

Personalize It!

The best way to vary these cookies is to flavor the ganache. Increase the cream by 2 tablespoons; heat it until small bubbles form around the sides of the pan. Add 2 Earl Grey tea bags; cover and steep for 20 minutes. Remove the tea bags and heat the cream a second time, as directed, before pouring over the chocolate.

Or stir any of the following into the cream before heating it: 1 tablespoon Cognac, 1 tablespoon Sambuca, 1 teaspoon instant espresso powder, 1 teaspoon maple flavoring, 1 teaspoon rum flavoring, or ½ teaspoon mint extract.

CHOCOLATE TUILES

Here's a crisp classic French cookie, reinvented with chocolate. Making tuiles requires a bit of a fuss, but they are an elegant, sophisticated dessert.

MAKES ABOUT 18 LARGE COOKIES

- ¼ cup all-purpose flour, plus additional for dusting the baking sheet
- 1 ounce bittersweet or semisweet chocolate, grated (see Chocolate Grater, page 15)
- ¼ cup slivered almonds
- ½ cup plus 1 tablespoon sugar
- 5 tablespoons cool, unsalted butter, cut into small pieces, plus additional for greasing the baking sheet
- 1 tablespoon milk (regular, low-fat, or nonfat)
- 1 tablespoon crème de cacao
- 2 large egg whites, lightly beaten

1. Position the rack in the center of the oven; preheat the oven to 425°F. Butter and flour a large baking sheet; set aside. Whisk the flour and grated chocolate in a small bowl until well combined; set aside as well, preferably out of the kitchen's heat.

2. Place the almonds and sugar in a food processor fitted with a chopping blade; pulse until finely ground, scraping down the sides of the bowl as necessary.

3. Place this almond mixture in a large bowl and cut in the butter, using a pastry cutter or two forks, until the mixture resembles coarse meal. Then beat with an electric mixer at medium speed until light and fluffy, about 1 minute. Beat in the milk and crème of cacao. Then beat in the egg whites in one-third increments, making sure each addition is incorporated before adding the next. Finally, remove the beaters and stir in the flour and chocolate mixture until moistened and evenly distributed.

4. Place 1 tablespoon of the batter on the prepared baking sheet, then use an offset spatula to spread it gently into a 2-inch circle. Repeat, making about 4 circles on the baking sheet.

5. Bake for about 6 minutes, or until soft but set. Cool on the baking sheet for 20 to 30 seconds, just until you can handle the cookies. Gently lift them off with a metal spatula, then lay them over a large rolling pin or a large plastic soda bottle, so that the cookies bend slightly into curved arcs. Let them rest in this position for about 3 minutes, or until set, then transfer to a wire rack, curved side down, and cool completely. Cool the baking sheet for about 5 minutes before buttering and flouring it a second time and making additional batches, or prepare a second baking sheet while the first is in the oven.

Recommended storage
2 days at room temperature
Not recommended for freezing

CLASSIC CHOCOLATE CHIP COOKIES

We've tweaked the classic recipe a bit—changing the ratio of the granulated and brown sugar to make a crisper cookie and adding far more chips than usual. We ask you this: What's the point of a chocolate chip cookie unless there's just enough batter to hold the chips in place?

MAKES ABOUT 5 DOZEN COOKIES

2¼	cups all-purpose flour
1	teaspoon baking soda
1	teaspoon salt
½	pound (2 sticks) cool, unsalted butter, cut into small pieces
1⅓	cups packed light brown sugar
½	cup granulated sugar
2	large eggs, at room temperature
2½	teaspoons vanilla extract
3	cups semisweet or bittersweet chocolate chips

1. Position the racks in the top and bottom thirds of the oven; preheat the oven to 375°F. Whisk the flour, baking soda, and salt in a medium bowl until uniform; set aside.

2. Soften the butter in a large bowl, using an electric mixer at medium speed, about 1 minute. Add both sugars and continue beating until light and airy, if still a bit grainy, a little more than 1 minute. Beat in the eggs one at a time, thoroughly beating in the first before adding the second. Scrape down the sides of the bowl, then beat in the vanilla. Remove the beaters.

3. Using a wooden spoon or a rubber spatula, fold in the prepared flour mixture just until moistened. The batter should be firm but not sticky. Fold in the chocolate chips just until evenly distributed. Drop by rounded tablespoons onto two ungreased baking sheets, preferably nonstick, spacing the mounds about 1½ inches apart.

4. Bake for 6 minutes, then switch the sheets top to bottom and back to front. Continue baking for about 6 more minutes, or until the cookies are lightly browned at the edges, set yet soft when touched. Cool on the baking sheets for 1 minute, then transfer the cookies to wire racks to cool completely. Cool the baking sheets for 5 minutes before baking additional batches.

Recommended storage
4 days at room temperature
3 months in the freezer

Customize It!

To make cakier cookies, refrigerate the dough for about 2 hours, or until somewhat stiff. Roll tablespoonfuls of the dough into balls and place them on the baking sheets, spacing them about 1½ inches apart. Do not press the balls down before baking.

Reduce the chocolate chips to 1½ cups and stir 1½ cups of any of the following, or any combination, into the batter with the remaining chocolate chips: butterscotch chips, chocolate-covered espresso beans, chocolate-covered peanuts, chocolate-covered raisins, chopped dried apricots, chopped dried pineapple, chopped hazelnuts, chopped Heath bars or Heath bar bits, chopped unsalted macadamia nuts, chopped pecans, chopped unsalted roasted cashews, chopped walnuts, dried cherries, dried cranberries, M&M's, mint chocolate chips, peanut butter chips, raisins, Reese's Pieces, unsweetened coconut chips, white chocolate chips.

COCONUT CHOCOLATE CHIP COOKIES

The hint of coconut in these cookies adds a tropical twist to the American classic.

MAKES ABOUT 3 DOZEN COOKIES

1	cup plus 1 tablespoon all-purpose flour
½	teaspoon baking soda
½	teaspoon salt
8	tablespoons (1 stick) cool, unsalted butter, cut into small pieces, plus additional for greasing the baking sheets
6	tablespoons solid vegetable shortening (3 ounces)
¾	cup packed light brown sugar
½	cup granulated sugar
1	large egg, at room temperature
½	teaspoon almond extract
1¾	cup unsweetened coconut chips (see page 19)
2	cups semisweet or bittersweet chocolate chips

1. Position the racks in the top and bottom thirds of the oven; preheat the oven to 350°F. Grease two large baking sheets with butter, using either the inside of the butter wrapper or a small sheet of crumpled wax paper dipped into softened butter; set the sheets aside. Whisk the flour, baking soda, and salt in a medium bowl until the baking soda is evenly distributed in the mixture; set aside as well.

2. Using an electric mixer at medium speed, soften and blend the butter and shortening in a large bowl until somewhat smooth, about 2 minutes. Add the brown sugar and granulated sugar and continue beating until fluffy and very pale brown, about 1 more minute. Beat in the egg and almond extract, then beat in the coconut just until evenly distributed. Remove the beaters.

3. Use a wooden spoon or a rubber spatula to mix in the prepared flour mixture just until moistened. Fold in the chocolate chips, using long, even arcs to incorporate them thoroughly into the batter without deflating it or causing it to become too sticky.

4. Drop by tablespoonfuls onto the prepared baking sheets. Bake for 7 minutes, then rotate the sheets top to bottom and front to back. Continue baking for about 6 more minutes, or until the cookies are lightly browned at the edges but still somewhat soft to the touch. Cool on the sheets for 5 minutes. Transfer to wire racks to continue cooling. Cool the baking sheets for 5 more minutes, then butter them again before proceeding with further batches, as necessary.

> **Recommended storage**
> *4 days at room temperature*
> *3 months in the freezer*

More Choices!

Coconut Banana Chocolate Chip Cookies: Reduce the chocolate chips to 1 cup; add 1 cup crushed banana chips with the remaining chocolate chips. Substitute banana flavoring for the almond extract.

Coconut Daiquiri Chocolate Chip Cookies: Add 2 tablespoons finely grated lime zest with the egg.

Coconut Pineapple Chocolate Chip Cookies: Reduce the chocolate chips to 1 cup; add 1 cup chopped dried pineapple with the remaining chocolate chips.

Coconut White Chocolate Chocolate Chip Cookies: Reduce the chocolate chips to 1 cup; add 1 cup white chocolate chips with the remaining chocolate chips.

Hawaiian Chocolate Chip Cookies: Reduce the chocolate chips to 1 cup; add ⅓ cup chopped dried pineapple, ⅓ cup chopped dried mango, ⅓ cup chopped dried papaya, and ⅓ cup unsalted macadamia nuts with the remaining chocolate chips.

Piña Colada Chocolate Chip Cookies: Reduce the chocolate chips to 1 cup; add 1 cup chopped dried pineapple with the remaining chocolate chips. Substitute 1 teaspoon rum flavoring for the almond extract. Substitute sweetened shredded coconut for the unsweetened coconut chips.

DAIRY-FREE CHOCOLATE CHIP COOKIES

To make dairy-free chocolate chip cookies, you just substitute margarine for butter in classic chocolate chip cookies, right? Actually, we found it takes a bit more finesse. Since margarine is "drier" than butter, it yields brittle cookies. To compensate, we've adjusted the sugar ratio, added rolled oats for better texture, and a touch of unsweetened coconut for moisture. The result? You won't miss the butter one bit.

MAKES ABOUT 5 DOZEN COOKIES

Nonstick spray

3	cups semisweet or bittersweet chocolate chips
1½	cups rolled oats (do not use quick-cooking oats)
½	cup unsweetened coconut chips (see page 19)
2	cups all-purpose flour
½	teaspoon baking soda
½	teaspoon salt
½	pound (2 sticks) cool margarine, cut into small pieces
1	cup granulated sugar
½	cup packed light brown sugar
1	large egg, at room temperature
2	teaspoons vanilla extract

1. Position the oven racks in the top and bottom thirds of the oven; preheat the oven to 350°F. Spray two large baking sheets with nonstick spray. Mix the chocolate chips, oats, and coconut chips in a medium bowl until well combined; set aside. Mix the flour, baking soda, and salt in a second medium bowl until uniform; set aside as well.

2. Soften the margarine slightly with an electric mixer at medium speed, then add both sugars, and beat until light, fluffy, and pale yellow, about 2 minutes, scraping down the sides of the bowl as necessary. Beat in the egg and vanilla, then remove the beaters. Pour in the prepared flour mixture all at once and stir with a wooden spoon or rubber spatula until there are no white streaks in the batter, although the batter may still have a slightly sandy look from the undissolved flour. Stir in the chocolate chip mixture just until well combined. The dough is quite stiff; you may need to work the chip mixture in by hand—just make sure you've washed your hands thoroughly.

3. Roll the dough into walnut-size balls, then place these on the prepared baking sheets about 1½ inches apart. Press the balls lightly with your fingers to flatten them slightly. Bake for 7 minutes, then rotate the baking sheets top to bottom, turning each front to back. Continue baking for about 8 more minutes, or until the cookies are lightly browned at the edges, with firm tops, but have some give if you touch them. Cool them on the baking sheets for 2 minutes, then transfer to wire racks and continue cooling. Let the baking sheets cool for 5 minutes before reusing them; spray them again with nonstick spray before baking additional batches.

Recommended storage
4 months at room temperature
3 months in the freezer

Customize It!
For a nutty dairy-free cookie, reduce the chocolate chips to 2 cups and add 1 cup of any of the following: chopped hazelnuts, chopped pecans, chopped roasted unsalted cashews, chopped roasted unsalted peanuts, chopped sliced almonds, chopped walnuts, or sesame seeds.

ESPRESSO CHOCOLATE CHIP BISCOTTI

For these biscotti, use only mini chocolate chips, or chop chocolate chips into bits that are no larger than one-third their original size. The technique here is a little different than some of the others in this book: you beat the sugar and eggs, then add melted butter for a slightly cakier consistency—in other words, these are biscotti that won't dry out so much, thereby compromising that espresso taste, turning the cookies bitter. Once you coat the logs in the egg-white wash, bake them immediately—if you wait, the wash will harden and the logs will crack too much at the sides when cut into cookies.

MAKES ABOUT 5 DOZEN SMALL BISCOTTI

2¼	cups all-purpose flour, plus additional for dusting
1½	teaspoons baking powder
¼	teaspoon salt
1	tablespoon vanilla extract
1½	tablespoons instant espresso powder
1	cup sugar
2	large eggs plus 1 large egg yolk, at room temperature
2	tablespoons unsalted butter, melted and cooled
1½	cups mini semisweet chocolate chips
1	large egg white, beaten in a small bowl with 1 teaspoon water until frothy

1. Position the rack in the center of the oven. Preheat the oven to 325°F. Line a large baking sheet with parchment paper or a silicone baking mat.

2. Whisk the flour, baking powder, and salt in a medium bowl until well combined. Place the vanilla in a small bowl or teacup; add the instant espresso powder and stir until fully dissolved. Set both mixtures aside.

3. In a large bowl, with an electric mixer at medium speed, beat the sugar, eggs, and egg yolk until light and pale yellow, about 2 minutes. Beat in the melted butter, then the vanilla-espresso mixture, just until smooth. Turn off the mixer, add the prepared flour mixture, and beat at low speed until a crumbly dough forms. Remove the beaters and pour in the chocolate chips; stir once or twice, just to distribute.

4. Lightly dust a clean, dry work surface with flour, then turn the dough out onto it. Knead for about 30 seconds until the dough holds together. It's quite full of chocolate chips, so keep reincorporating any chips that fall out. Divide the dough in half, then shape into two logs about 10 inches long. Flatten each to a cylinder about 1 inch high at its apex. Transfer the logs to the prepared baking sheet, placing them about 4 inches apart.

5. Brush each log with the egg-white wash, then bake for 45 minutes, or until light brown and quite firm to the touch. The tops will be shiny and the sides a bit cracked. Cool on the baking sheet for about 30 minutes, or until easily handled.

6. Transfer the logs to a cutting board and use a serrated knife to slice each into small cookies a little more than ¼ inch thick. If desired, slice on the diagonal, thereby making longer cookies. Place the cookies, cut side down, on the prepared baking sheet, spacing them about ¼ inch apart. If the baking sheet will not hold them all, reserve the rest for a second baking after the first has finished.

7. Bake for 7 minutes, then flip them over to the other cut side. Continue baking for about 7 more minutes, or until lightly toasted and quite dry but not too hard (they will crisp as they cool). Transfer to a wire rack to cool completely. If you're baking additional batches, replace the parchment paper if it's frizzled, browned, or torn.

> ***Recommended storage***
> *5 days at room temperature*
> *2 months in the freezer once baked*

Personalize It!
You can dip these biscotti in melted chocolate, following the technique for dipped Chocolate Biscotti on page 46. For a more pronounced chocolate taste, stir 1½ tablespoons Kahlúa or other coffee-flavored liqueur into the cooled, melted chocolate before dipping the biscotti in it.

FRENCH MACAROONS

In our version of this Parisian classic, two crunchy almond macaroons sandwich a smooth layer of melted chocolate. They're fussy, fancy, and ever so good.

MAKES ABOUT 3 DOZEN SMALL SANDWICH COOKIES

One 7-ounce tube almond paste (see page 17)
1 cup sugar
⅛ teaspoon salt
2 large egg whites, at room temperature
3 ounces semisweet chocolate

1. Position the rack in the center of the oven; preheat the oven to 375°F. Line a large baking sheet with parchment paper or a silicone baking mat; set aside.

2. Beat the almond paste and sugar in a large bowl with an electric mixer at slow speed until the almond paste has broken up and begins to incorporate the sugar; increase the speed to medium and continue beating until the mixture looks like fine meal, about 5 minutes. Scrape down the sides of the bowl and beat in the salt.

3. Beat in the egg whites one at time, taking care that the first is incorporated into the batter before adding the second. In the end, the batter should look fairly creamy but still somewhat grainy.

4. Fit a pastry bag with a round, ¾-inch tip; fill the bag with the almond mixture and pipe it out onto the prepared baking sheet, making small dots with about 1 teaspoon of the batter, spacing them about 1 inch apart. Flatten the disks somewhat as you pipe them out, then swirl the tip at the finish to create a little cowlick of batter. You can forgo the pastry bag and drop teaspoonfuls of dough onto the prepared sheet, but take care to make small, compact mounds, much like a tiny, smushed Hershey's Kiss.

5. Bake for 10 minutes, or until lightly browned. Cool the cookies completely on the baking sheet before removing them to a wire rack. Repeat the baking process with any unused batter, replacing the parchment paper if it is dry or browned.

6. When the cookies are cool, place the chocolate in the top half of a double boiler set over a pot with about 1 inch of simmering water, or place the chocolate in a medium bowl that fits securely over a medium saucepan with about the same amount of simmering water. Stir until half the chocolate has melted, then remove the top half of the double boiler or the bowl from the heat and continue stirring until all the chocolate has melted. Cool for 5 minutes.

7. Smear 1 teaspoon of melted chocolate on the flat bottom of one of the cookies, then press the flat bottom of a second cookie against the chocolate, thereby making a small sandwich cookie. Place the filled cookies on a wire rack to allow the chocolate to firm up at room temperature, about 1 hour. Repeat with the remaining cookies and chocolate.

Recommended storage
2 days at room temperature
Not recommended for freezing

Customize It!
Substitute bittersweet, milk, or white chocolate for the semisweet chocolate. You can flavor the milk or white chocolate with 1 tablespoon of any of the following: amaretto or other almond liqueur, Chambord or other raspberry liqueur, Cognac, dark rum, Grand Marnier or other orange liqueur, Kahlúa or other coffee liqueur, Original Canton Delicate Ginger Liqueur or other ginger liqueur, or a single-malt whiskey.

FRIED CHOCOLATE COOKIES

Pierre Reboul, the pastry chef at New York's fabulous Blue Hill restaurant, was the genius behind the batter for these deep-fried cookies. Not for every day, these treats are a one-in-a-million shot at utter decadence.

MAKES ABOUT 2 DOZEN DECADENT COOKIES

- ½ cup warm water, between 105°F and 115°F
- 2 tablespoons unsalted butter, melted and cooled to between 105°F and 115°F
- One ¾-ounce package dry yeast
- 3 large eggs, at room temperature
- One 12-ounce bottle beer, preferably a pale ale or a weissbeer, at room temperature
- 2½ cups all-purpose flour
- ½ cup plus 1 tablespoon cocoa powder, sifted
- ⅓ cup sugar
- 1 teaspoon salt
- 6 cups canola oil or vegetable oil
- 24 Mallomars or Oreo cookies

1. Combine the water and melted butter in a large bowl. Stir in the yeast. Let stand for 2 minutes, just to dissolve the yeast.

2. Whisk in the eggs one at a time, then gently stir in the beer, just until the foam subsides. Use a wooden spoon to stir in the flour, cocoa powder, sugar, and salt, just until uniform, if still a little grainy. Cover the bowl with plastic wrap and place in the refrigerator overnight, at least 12 hours but not more than 24 hours, until the mixture rises somewhat and is about the consistency of pudding.

3. Pour the oil into a 3-quart saucepan or pot and attach a deep-frying thermometer to the inside of the pan. Heat the oil over medium heat until it reaches 350°F. Alternatively, you can use a deep-fryer; add the oil and follow the manufacturer's instructions for heating it. While the oil is heating, take the prepared chocolate batter out of the refrigerator and let it sit at room temperature.

4. Dip a cookie deep into the batter. Hold it up to let some of the batter drip back into the bowl, but make sure the cookie is completely coated. Slip the coated cookie into the hot oil. Continue dipping the cookies until the pan holds as many as it can without crowding, probably 4 or 5 cookies. Adjust the heat so that the oil stays at a constant 350°F. Fry for about 30 seconds, using a wire-mesh skimmer or a long-handled slotted metal spoon to turn the cookies in the oil and brown them on all sides. When puffed and somewhat stiff, remove the fried cookies from the oil and drain them on a plate lined with paper towels. Repeat this process until all the cookies are dipped and fried. If desired, form any excess batter into small lumps, using two spoons to mound it together, and then fry these bundles in the oil.

Recommended storage
No more than 12 hours at room temperature
Not recommended for freezing

Personalize It!

You can experiment with your favorite cookies, such as sugar wafers, purchased pecan sandies, or peanut butter sandwich cookies. Almost any sandwich cookie will work; but steer clear of graham crackers, meringues, or biscotti.

FUDGE MERINGUES

Unlike traditional, stiff-peaked meringue cookies, these are flat, round, and so loaded with chocolate that they can barely stand up. A little crisp on the outside, they're ooey-gooey inside—irresistible and luscious.

MAKES ABOUT 3 DOZEN MERINGUE COOKIES

1	ounce unsweetened chocolate, chopped
¼	cup cocoa powder, sifted
¼	cup confectioners' sugar
1	tablespoon cornstarch
3	large egg whites, at room temperature
⅛	teaspoon salt
⅛	teaspoon cream of tartar
⅔	cup granulated sugar
1	tablespoon vanilla extract, or less to taste

1. Place the chocolate in a large bowl and microwave on high for 15 seconds. Stir well, then continue heating on high in 15-second increments, stirring after each, until half the chocolate has melted. Remove the bowl from the microwave oven and continue stirring until the chocolate has completely melted. Alternatively, place the chocolate in the top half of a double boiler set over about 1 inch of simmering water; stir until half the chocolate has melted, then remove from the heat and continue stirring until the chocolate has fully melted. In either case, cool the melted chocolate for 5 minutes.

2. Meanwhile, position the rack in the center of the oven; preheat the oven to 300°F. Line a large baking sheet with parchment paper or a silicone baking mat. Mix the cocoa powder, confectioners' sugar, and cornstarch in a medium bowl until a uniform color; set aside.

3. In a large, scrupulously dry bowl, using an electric mixer at medium speed, beat the egg whites and salt until foamy. Add the cream of tartar; continue beating until soft peaks form, about 2 minutes. Beat in the granulated sugar 1 tablespoon at a time, adding each in a slow, steady stream. Once all the sugar has been added, continue beating for about 6 minutes, or until you can't feel any sugar grains when you rub the mixture between your fingers.

4. Beat in the cooled, melted chocolate until smooth, then use a rubber spatula to fold in the prepared cocoa mixture just until moistened. Do not deflate the egg whites; fold in slow, easy strokes, just until evenly distributed.

5. Scoop up leveled teaspoonfuls of the batter and gently mound them on the prepared baking sheet, spacing them about 1½ inches apart. Bake until the cookies are slightly spread and the tops are dry to the touch, 20 to 25 minutes. Refrigerate any unused batter for a second baking. Cool for 3 minutes on the sheets, then carefully transfer the fragile meringues to a wire rack to cool completely. Cool the baking sheet for at least 5 minutes before baking a second batch.

Recommended storage
3 days at room temperature
Not recommended for freezing

Mix It Up!
Espresso Fudge Meringues: Use the vanilla extract to make a paste with ½ teaspoon instant espresso powder, stirring until dissolved. Fold this mixture into the batter as you would the plain vanilla.

Ginger Fudge Meringues: Add 1 teaspoon ground ginger with the flour.

Rum Fudge Meringues: Reduce the vanilla extract to 2 teaspoons; add 1 teaspoon rum flavoring with the remaining vanilla.

GANACHE THUMBPRINTS

These cookies are much like traditional thumbprint cookies, buttery and studded with pecans, but the centers are filled with a rich dark chocolate ganache.

MAKES ABOUT 2 DOZEN COOKIES

- 2 cups all-purpose flour
- ½ teaspoon baking soda
- ½ teaspoon salt
- 2 cups very finely chopped pecans
- 3 ounces semisweet chocolate, chopped
- ⅓ cup heavy cream
- ½ pound (2 sticks) cool, unsalted butter, cut into small pieces, plus additional for greasing the baking sheets
- ½ cup packed light brown sugar
- 2 large egg yolks, at room temperature
- 2 teaspoons vanilla extract
- 2 large egg whites, beaten in a small bowl with 2 tablespoons water until frothy

1. Position the rack in the center of the oven. Preheat the oven to 375°F.

2. Begin by preparing things you will need as you move through the recipe. Lightly butter a large baking sheet; set it aside. Whisk the flour, baking soda, and salt in a medium bowl; set aside. Place the pecans on a large plate. To make the ganache, place the chocolate in a medium bowl, then heat the cream in a medium saucepan just until small bubbles form around the edges of the pan. Pour the heated cream over the chocolate and stir until melted and smooth, if a little runny (it will become firm as the cookies cool). Set the chocolate aside and prepare the cookies.

3. Soften the butter in a large bowl, using an electric mixer at medium speed, about 1 minute. Add the brown sugar and beat at medium speed until pale yellow and very soft, about 2 minutes. Beat in the egg yolks one at a time, then the vanilla until smooth. Turn off the beaters, add the prepared flour mixture, and beat at low speed just until a soft dough forms with some floury grains still present.

4. Roll a level tablespoon of the dough between your palms. Roll this ball in the egg-white mixture, then into the chopped pecans, studding the outside with the nuts. Place on the prepared baking sheet and repeat until the sheet is filled, spacing the balls about 1½ inches apart.

5. Bake for 5 minutes. Remove from the oven and make an indentation in each cookie, either by wetting your thumb and pressing it into the cookie, or by using the handle of a wooden spoon. (See Chocolate Jam Thumbprints, page 99, for a more detailed explanation of this process.) Fill each indentation with 1 teaspoon of the prepared ganache.

6. Bake for another 10 minutes, or until the cookies are lightly browned at the edges and the chocolate center just starts to bubble around the edges. Cool for 2 minutes on the baking sheet, then use a metal spatula to transfer the cookies to a wire rack to cool completely. Cool the baking sheet for 5 minutes and butter it again before making more cookies—or use a second, buttered baking sheet that hasn't been in the oven.

Recommended storage
4 days between sheets of wax paper
Not recommended for freezing

Customize It!
Flavor the ganache by stirring 1½ tablespoons of any of the following into the cooled, melted chocolate mixture: Amaretto or other almond liqueur, Chambord or other raspberry liqueur, Frangelico or other hazelnut liqueur, Grand Marnier or other orange liqueur, Kahlúa or other coffee-flavored liqueur, or Oh Canada Maple Liqueur or other maple liqueur.

GINGER CHOCOLATE CHIP COOKIES

Here's a chocolate chip cookie spiked with both ground and crystallized ginger, and made a little chewier thanks to molasses and an extra egg white. Call them a cross between a classic chocolate cookie and gingerbread. If you prefer chewier cookies, remove them from the oven while they're still quite soft.

MAKES A LITTLE MORE THAN 3 DOZEN COOKIES

2⅓	cups all-purpose flour
1	tablespoon ground ginger
1	teaspoon baking soda
½	teaspoon grated nutmeg
½	teaspoon salt
½	pound (2 sticks) cool, unsalted butter, cut into small pieces
1	cup granulated sugar
½	cup packed dark brown sugar
2	tablespoons molasses, preferably unsulphured
1	large egg, at room temperature
1	large egg white, at room temperature
2	teaspoons vanilla extract
¾	cup finely chopped crystallized ginger
3	cups semisweet or bittersweet chocolate chips, or chocolate chunks

1. Position the racks in the top and bottom thirds of the oven; preheat the oven to 350°F. Whisk the flour, ground ginger, baking soda, nutmeg, and salt in a medium bowl until uniform; set aside.

2. Use an electric mixer at medium speed to soften the butter in a large bowl, just until smooth and light, about 2 minutes. Add the granulated sugar, brown sugar, and molasses; continue beating until fluffy, if still a little grainy, about 2 more minutes. Beat in the egg, then the egg white, and then the vanilla until smooth. Beat in the crystallized ginger at low speed just until evenly distributed. Turn off the beaters, add the prepared flour mixture (in stages, if necessary), and beat at a very low speed just until a soft, creamy dough forms.

3. Drop by scant tablespoonfuls onto two large, ungreased baking sheets, preferably nonstick, spacing the mounds about 2 inches apart. Bake for 7 minutes, then reverse the sheets back to front and top to bottom. Continue baking for about 6 more minutes, or until the cookies are slightly puffed, set, but still soft. Cool on the baking sheets for 3 minutes, then transfer the cookies to wire racks to cool completely. Cool the baking sheets for 5 minutes before baking additional batches, as necessary.

Recommended storage
3 days at room temperature
3 months in the freezer

More Choices!

Almond Ginger Chocolate Chip Cookies: Reduce the chocolate chips to 2 cups; add 1 cup sliced almonds with the remaining chips.

Chestnut Ginger Chocolate Chip Cookies: Reduce the chocolate chips to 1½ cups; add 1½ cups chopped roasted peeled chestnuts with the remaining chips.

Lemon Ginger Chocolate Chip Cookies: Substitute ½ cup finely chopped candied lemon rind for the crystallized ginger.

Walnut Ginger Chocolate Chip Cookies: Reduce the chocolate chips to 2 cups; add 1 cup chopped walnuts with the remaining chips.

GLUTEN-FREE CHOCOLATE CHIP COOKIES

You might think the only reason to make these specialty cookies is because you or someone you know is on a gluten-restricted diet—but you'd be wrong. These are soft, moist cookies, a little crumbly and very good with cup of strong coffee. Still and all, they're perfect for anyone who wants to cut down on flour, whether by choice or for health reasons. Soft, moist, and a little crumbly, they're perfect with a cup of strong coffee.

MAKES ABOUT 3½ DOZEN COOKIES

1½	cups plus 2 tablespoons white rice flour (see Note)
¼	cup potato starch (see Note)
1	tablespoon xanthan gum (see Note)
½	teaspoon baking soda
½	teaspoon salt
8	tablespoons (1 stick) cool, unsalted butter, cut into small pieces
8	tablespoons (1 stick) cool margarine, cut into small pieces
½	cup granulated sugar
½	cup packed dark brown sugar
2	large eggs, at room temperature
1	teaspoon gluten-free vanilla flavoring
2	cups gluten-free chocolate chips, or semisweet chocolate chips

1. Position the rack in the top third of the oven. Preheat the oven to 350°F. Whisk the rice flour, potato starch, xanthan gum, baking soda, and salt in a medium bowl until well combined; set aside.

2. Soften the butter and margarine in a large bowl, using an electric mixer at medium speed, about 1 minute. Add both kinds of sugar and continue beating until light and fluffy, about 2 minutes. Beat in the eggs one at a time, making sure the first is fully incorporated before adding the second. Beat in the vanilla until smooth.

3. Remove the beaters and use a wooden spoon or a rubber spatula to stir in the prepared rice flour mixture, just until moistened. Stir in the chocolate chips until evenly distributed. Let stand at room temperature for 5 minutes.

4. Drop by scant tablespoonfuls onto a large ungreased baking sheet, preferably nonstick, spacing the mounds 2 inches apart. Bake in the top third of the oven for 14 minutes, rotating the sheet back to front halfway through baking. When done, the cookies should be lightly browned and set, although soft to the touch. Cool on the baking sheet for 3 minutes, then use a metal spatula to transfer the soft, fragile cookies to a wire rack to cool completely. Cool the baking sheet for 5 minutes before baking additional batches, or use a baking sheet that hasn't already been in the oven.

NOTE: *White rice flour, potato starch, and xanthan gum are available at most gourmet supermarkets and almost all health food stores. Make sure you buy white rice flour—not brown rice or glutinous rice flour. Xanthan gum is a corn-based derivative that stabilizes the dough—in the absence of the glutens, it allows the cookies to hold their shape after they're baked. If you read labels, you know it's a common ingredient in low-fat, nonfat, and gluten-free baked goods.*

Recommended storage:
3 days at room temperature
2 months in the freezer

Make It Yours!
Reduce the chocolate chips to 1 cup; add 1 cup of any of the following with the remaining chips: chopped dried figs, chopped dried strawberries, chopped pecans, chopped pitted dates, chopped roasted unsalted cashews, chopped roasted unsalted peanuts, chopped unsalted macadamia nuts, chopped unsalted pistachios, chopped walnuts, dried blueberries, dried cherries, dried cranberries, or raisins.

HONEY CHOCOLATE CHIP COOKIES

For the best taste, use a strong-flavored honey in this otherwise traditional recipe: for example, wildflower, pine tree, oak tree, acacia, chestnut, or (our favorite) star thistle. Gourmet markets and even some supermarkets regularly stock these varietals—or check out our recommendations in the Source Guide, page 229.

MAKES ABOUT 5 DOZEN COOKIES

2½	cups all-purpose flour
1	cup rolled oats (do not use quick-cooking oats)
½	teaspoon baking soda
½	teaspoon salt
½	pound (2 sticks) unsalted butter, at room temperature
½	cup honey (see Note)
1	teaspoon vanilla
3	cups semisweet or bittersweet chocolate chips

1. Whisk the flour, oats, baking soda, and salt in a medium bowl until uniform; set aside.

2. Soften the butter in a large bowl, using an electric mixer at medium speed, about 1 minute. Add the honey and vanilla; continue beating until thick and creamy, about 2 minutes. Turn off the beaters, add the prepared flour mixture (in batches, if necessary), and beat at low speed just until a wet, soft dough is formed. Stir in the chocolate chips. Let the dough stand at room temperature for 30 minutes before proceeding.

3. Meanwhile, position the racks in the top and bottom thirds of the oven; preheat the oven to 325°F.

4. Drop by rounded teaspoonfuls onto two large, ungreased baking sheets, preferably nonstick, spacing the mounds about 1½ inches apart. Bake for 8 minutes, then rotate the baking sheets top to bottom and back to front. Bake for another 4 minutes, then flatten the cookies with the back of a flatware spoon, especially if they've begun to puff up. Bake for about 4 more minutes, or until lightly browned and somewhat firm to the touch. Cool on the baking sheets for 2 minutes, then transfer the cookies to wire racks to cool completely. Let the sheets cool for 5 minutes before baking further batches.

NOTE: *To liquefy crystallized honey, place the jar in a large bowl and fill the bowl with hot water until it comes up to within 1 inch of the jar's lip; let stand for 10 minutes. Repeat if the honey has not fully liquefied.*

Recommended storage
5 days at room temperature
3 months in the freezer

Mix It Up!

Cashew Honey Chocolate Chip Cookies: Omit the salt. Reduce the chocolate chips to 2 cups; add 1 cup chopped roasted salted cashews with the remaining chips.

Peanut Butter and Banana Honey Chocolate Chip Cookies: Reduce the chocolate chips to 1 cup; add 1 cup crushed banana chips and 1 cup peanut butter chips with the remaining chips.

Seeds and Honey Chocolate Chip Cookies: Reduce the chocolate chips to 1½ cups; add ½ cup sesame seeds, ½ cup unsalted sunflower seeds, and ½ cup pumpkin seeds with the remaining chips.

Walnut Honey Chocolate Chip Cookies: Reduce the chocolate chips to 2 cups; add 1 cup chopped walnut pieces with the remaining chips.

LOW-FAT CHOCOLATE BISCOTTI

The only fat in these cookies is in the almonds, which give the cookie a crack without using any butter. We've added dried cherries to keep the cookies moist—but check out the variations for endless possibilities. We prefer Dutch-processed cocoa powder in this recipe; it won't scorch and turn bitter during the long baking time.

MAKES ABOUT 2 DOZEN COOKIES

2	cups all-purpose flour, plus additional for dusting
1	cup sugar
½	cup cocoa powder, preferably Dutch-processed, sifted
1	teaspoon baking powder
½	teaspoon ground cinnamon
½	teaspoon baking soda
¼	teaspoon salt
¾	cup pasteurized egg substitute, such as Egg Beaters
1	tablespoon vanilla extract
½	cup whole almonds
½	cup dried cherries

1. Arrange the rack in the center of the oven; preheat the oven to 350°F. Line a large baking sheet with parchment paper or a silicone baking mat.

2. Whisk the flour, sugar, cocoa powder, baking powder, cinnamon, baking soda, and salt in a medium bowl until uniform. Stir in the egg substitute and vanilla with a wooden spoon, then stir in the almonds and cherries. The dough will be like a very dry biscuit dough, far drier than a piecrust.

3. Make sure your work surface is clean and scrupulously dry. Dust it with flour, then turn the dough out onto it. Knead for a few turns to get the almonds and cherries evenly distributed. Don't overwork the dough or let it get elastic—quit when it holds together as a rather dry but pliable ball. Divide the dough in half and roll into two logs, each about 16 inches long and 1 inch thick.

4. Place the logs on the prepared baking sheet and bake for about 25 minutes, or until somewhat firm. Cool the logs on the baking sheet until room temperature, at least 40 minutes.

5. Place the logs on a cutting board and use a serrated knife to slice them into ¾-inch cookies. If you cut on the diagonal, the individual cookies will be longer. If you've used parchment paper, line the baking sheet with a new piece if the used one is torn or singed. Place the cookies, cut side down, on the prepared baking sheet, only ¼ inch apart. If they don't all fit on the sheet, reserve the rest of the cookies for a second baking when the first batch is finished.

6. Bake for 8 minutes. Turn them over so the other cut side is against the sheet and continue baking for about 8 more minutes, or until lightly toasted and hard. Cool them on the baking sheet for 10 minutes, then transfer to a wire rack and cool completely.

Recommended storage
1 week at room temperature
3 months in the freezer

Customize It!
Substitute any of the following for the dried cherries: currants, dried blueberries, dried cranberries, or golden raisins.

And/or substitute any of the following for the almonds: pecan halves, walnut halves, or whole hazelnuts.

MAPLE CHOCOLATE CHIP COOKIES

The secret ingredient in these intensely flavored chocolate chip cookies is maple sugar. Maple syrup, even Grade B (the strongest flavor), simply doesn't pack enough punch to stand up to the chocolate. Maple sugar is dehydrated maple syrup, and can be found in most gourmet stores or from outlets listed in the Source Guide, page 229.

MAKES ABOUT 3 DOZEN COOKIES

1¾	cups all-purpose flour
½	teaspoon baking soda
½	teaspoon salt
12	tablespoons (1½ sticks) cool, unsalted butter, cut into small pieces, plus additional for greasing the baking sheets
1½	cups maple sugar
2	large eggs, at room temperature
1	teaspoon vanilla extract
2½	cups semisweet or bittersweet chocolate chips

1. Position the racks in the top and bottom thirds of the oven; preheat the oven to 350°F. Lightly butter two large baking sheets; set them aside. Whisk the flour, baking soda, and salt in a medium bowl until the baking soda is uniform throughout the mixture; set aside as well.

2. Soften the butter in a large bowl, using an electric mixer at medium speed, about 1 minute. Add the maple sugar and beat until light, pale brown, and fluffy, about 2 minutes. Scrape down the sides of the bowl, then add the eggs one at a time, beating the first in before adding the second. Beat in the vanilla. Turn off the beaters, add the prepared flour mixture, and beat at low speed just until incorporated. Stir in the chocolate chips with a wooden spoon. The batter will be thick and sticky, but don't press down as you stir in the chips—you want to retain a light, moist batter.

3. Drop by rounded tablespoonfuls onto the prepared baking sheets. Bake for 6 minutes, then rotate the sheets top to bottom and back to front. Continue baking for about 6 more minutes, or until the cookies are lightly browned and slightly puffed—if you touch one, it will be a little soft, but the indentation will remain in the cookie. Cool on the sheets for 3 minutes, then transfer to wire racks to cool completely. Cool the baking sheets for 5 minutes before buttering them again and baking additional batches, as needed.

Recommended storage
4 days at room temperature
3 months in the freezer

More Choices!

For cakier cookies, refrigerate the dough for about 2 hours, or until firm. Roll tablespoonfuls of the chilled dough into small balls and place them on the prepared baking sheets, spacing them about 1½ inches apart. Bake as directed, pressing them lightly wih a flatware spoon halfway through baking.

For still cakier cookies, roll tablespoonfuls of the chilled dough into balls and freeze the balls for 8 hours, or until hard. Bake them directly from the freezer, placing them on the prepared baking sheets and spacing them about 1½ inches apart. Increase the baking time by 1 to 2 minutes.

MEXICAN CHOCOLATE WALNUT COOKIES

This is our chocolate version of Mexican Wedding Cakes—crispy little nut cookies, often coated in powdered sugar and served at Christmas or on special occasions. The fat in the chocolate will cause them to flatten somewhat, instead of keeping their traditional, mounded shape; but they'll be just as crisp and nutty. We've used Mexican chocolate, a special variety made with ground almonds, spices, and sometimes ground cocoa nibs. Look for brands like Ibarra in their traditional hexagonal boxes at gourmet markets and specialty baking stores.

MAKES A LITTLE LESS THAN 4 DOZEN COOKIES

- ½ pound (2 sticks) cool, unsalted butter, cut into small pieces
- 1 cup confectioners' sugar
- 1 teaspoon vanilla extract
- ¼ teaspoon salt
- ¾ cup walnut pieces, finely ground in a food processor
- 1¾ cups all-purpose flour
- 6½ ounces Mexican chocolate, such as 2 rounds of Lbarra, grated with the small holes of a box grater

1. Position the rack in the center of the oven and preheat the oven to 350°F.

2. Soften the butter in a large bowl, using an electric mixer at medium speed, about 1 minute. Add the confectioners' sugar and beat until soft and creamy, if still a little grainy, about 1 more minute. Beat in the vanilla and salt, then the ground nuts, just until combined. Remove the beaters and stir in the flour and grated Mexican chocolate with a wooden spoon or a rubber spatula just until moistened. The dough will be soft, but will hold together. Form it into a ball, flatten slightly, wrap in plastic wrap, and refrigerate for about 1 hour just until firm but not hard.

3. Unwrap the dough, pinch off walnut-size pieces, and roll into balls. Place them about 2 inches apart on a large, ungreased baking sheet, preferably nonstick.

Reseal any unused dough in plastic wrap and refrigerate until you're ready to use it.

4. Bake for about 15 minutes, rotating the sheet back to front halfway through baking, until the cookies are flattened somewhat but still a little bumpy, set but still soft. Cool for 2 minutes on the baking sheet, then transfer to a wire rack to cool completely. Cool the baking sheet for 5 minutes, or use one that hasn't been in the oven, to continue baking additional batches.

Recommended storage
4 days at room temperature
2 months in the freezer

Dipped Mexican Chocolate Cookies
Place 12 ounces bittersweet, semisweet, milk, or white chocolate in the top half of a double boiler set over simmering water, or a medium bowl set over a saucepan with a small amount of simmering water; stir until half the chocolate has melted, then remove from the heat and continue stirring until all the chocolate has melted. Cool for 5 minutes. Dip the cooled cookies into the chocolate, then place the cookies on a wire rack set on wax paper for about 30 minutes, until the chocolate coating hardens.

MOLE COOKIES

Okay, we'll admit it up front: these aren't for everyone. They have the taste of mole, a traditional Mexican sauce—sesame seeds, pepitas (pumpkin seeds), ground chiles, cinnamon, and cloves. What's more, we've stacked the cookies with two kinds of chocolate for a sophisticated taste. They're aromatic at first bite, then the heat starts to build. Try them with a scoop of cooling raspberry sorbet.

MAKES ABOUT 3½ DOZEN COOKIES

1¾	cups all-purpose flour
2	tablespoons cocoa powder, sifted
½	teaspoon ground cinnamon
¼	teaspoon ground cloves
¼	teaspoon salt
½	cup pepitas (see Note)
¼	cup sesame seeds, lightly toasted
3	ounces unsweetened chocolate, chopped
¾	cup solid vegetable shortening (6 ounces)
2	tablespoons cool, unsalted butter, cut into small pieces
½	cup granulated sugar
¼	cup packed light brown sugar
2	large egg yolks, at room temperature
1	teaspoon vanilla extract
⅔	cup dried currants
1½	cups finely chopped pecan pieces

1. Position the racks in the top and bottom thirds of the oven; preheat the oven to 350°F. Whisk the flour, cocoa powder, cinnamon, cloves, and salt in a large bowl until evenly colored; set aside. Place the pepitas and sesame seeds in a food processor fitted with the chopping blade; process until finely ground; set aside, too.

2. Place the chocolate in the top half of a double boiler set over about 2 inches of simmering water, or in a medium bowl that fits snugly over a medium pot with about the same amount of simmering water. Stir until half the chocolate has melted, then remove the double boiler's top half or the bowl from the heat and continue stirring until the chocolate has fully melted. Cool for 5 minutes.

3. Meanwhile, soften the shortening and butter in a large bowl, using an electric mixer at medium speed. Add both kinds of sugar; continue beating until airy and light, if still a little gritty, about 1 minute. Beat in the egg yolks one at a time, making sure the first is incorporated before adding the second; beat in the melted chocolate and vanilla until smooth. Beat in the ground sesame seeds and pepitas, then remove the beaters and scrape down the sides of the bowl.

4. Use a wooden spoon or rubber spatula to stir in the prepared flour mixture just until moistened. Stir in the currants. The dough will be soft but a little greasy; turn it out onto a clean work surface and knead it three or four times, just until it adheres into a ball.

5. Spread the chopped pecans on a large plate. Pinch off a walnut-size piece of dough; then flatten it into the chopped pecans, pressing down so that only one side is coated with the nuts and the dough is shaped like a flattened basketball. Place the ball, pecan side up, on an ungreased baking sheet, then continue this process, filling two large baking sheets with cookies, spacing them about 1½ inches apart.

6. Bake for 6 minutes, then reverse the sheets back to front and top to bottom. Bake for about 6 more minutes, or until the cookies are a bit cracked yet still somewhat soft to the touch but very aromatic. Cool for 3 minutes on the baking sheets, then transfer to wire racks to cool completely. Cool the baking sheets for 5 minutes before baking additional batches as needed.

NOTE: *Pepitas are pumpkin seeds, often green because they've been hulled, sometimes toasted. They're available in some health food stores, most gourmet markets, and almost all Latin American markets.*

Recommended storage
4 days at room temperature
3 months in the freezer

NEARLY NONFAT CHOCOLATE COOKIES

The only fat in these cookies is in the tiny amount of cocoa butter left in the unsweetened chocolate, and in the minuscule residual amount in the cocoa powder. Other than that, there's no butter or shortening—although the cookies are so soft and moist, you won't believe it.

MAKES ABOUT 2 DOZEN LARGE COOKIES

- 1 cup all-purpose flour
- 2 tablespoons cocoa powder, preferably natural, sifted
- ½ teaspoon baking soda
- ½ teaspoon salt
- 2 ounces unsweetened chocolate, chopped
- 4 large egg whites, at room temperature
- 1 cup packed dark brown sugar
- ½ cup granulated sugar
- 1 teaspoon vanilla extract

1. Position the rack in the middle of the oven; preheat the oven to 350°F. Line a large baking sheet with parchment paper or a silicone baking mat; set aside. Whisk the flour, cocoa powder, baking soda, and salt in a medium bowl until uniform; set aside as well.

2. Place the chocolate in the top half of a double boiler set over about 1 inch of simmering water, or in a medium bowl that fits securely over a medium saucepan with about the same amount of simmering water. Stir until half the chocolate has melted, then remove from the double boiler's top half or the bowl from the heat and continue stirring until all the chocolate has melted. Alternatively, place the chocolate in a medium bowl and microwave on high in 15-second increments until half the chocolate has melted, then continue stirring at room temperature until all the chocolate has melted. In all cases, set aside to cool for 5 minutes.

3. Meanwhile, place the egg whites in a large bowl and beat with an electric mixer at medium speed until foamy, about 20 seconds. Add both kinds of sugar and beat until thick and smooth, about 3 minutes at medium speed. Pour in the cooled, melted chocolate and continue beating until uniform, then beat in the vanilla. Remove the beaters and stir in the prepared flour mixture with a wooden spoon or a metal spatula, just until the flour is moistened and evenly distributed. Do not over-beat or the dough will be too sticky.

4. Drop by rounded tablespoonfuls onto the prepared baking sheet. Bake for 12 minutes, switching the sheet back to front halfway through baking, until the cookies are flat yet springy with crackly, dry-looking tops. Cool on the baking sheet for 3 minutes, then transfer them to a wire rack and cool completely. Cool the baking sheet for 5 minutes before baking additional batches.

Recommended storage
4 days at room temperature
1 month in the freezer

Personalize It!

Stir in ⅔ cup of any of the following with the vanilla extract: golden raisins, currants, chopped dried apricots, chopped dried figs, or chopped dried pineapple.

Substitute any of the following for the vanilla extract: 1 teaspoon banana flavoring, 1 teaspoon coconut flavoring, 1 teaspoon orange extract, ½ teaspoon mint flavoring, 1 teaspoon rum flavoring.

PEANUT BUTTER CHOCOLATE CHIP COOKIES

The problem with peanut butter chocolate chip cookies? Well, none, except they're often too soft for our taste. So we've taken the egg yolks out of the batter, thereby making these cookies crunchy and irresistible. There's just enough rich peanut butter dough to hold all the chocolate chips in place. No problem there at all.

MAKES ABOUT 3½ DOZEN COOKIES

1½	cups all-purpose flour
¾	teaspoon baking soda
½	teaspoon salt
4	tablespoons (½ stick) cool, unsalted butter, cut into small pieces
¾	cup creamy peanut butter
¼	cup solid vegetable shortening (2 ounces)
1	cup granulated sugar
¼	cup packed dark brown sugar
2	large egg whites, at room temperature
1	tablespoon vanilla extract
3	cups semisweet chocolate chips

1. Position the rack in the center of the oven. Preheat the oven to 375°F. Whisk the flour, baking soda, and salt in a medium bowl until uniform; set aside.

2. Soften the butter in a large bowl, using an electric mixer at medium speed. Add the peanut butter and shortening; beat until smooth, about 1 minute. Then beat in the granulated sugar and brown sugar until light, fluffy, but still a little coarsely textured, about 1 more minute. Beat in the egg whites and vanilla until smooth. Turn off the mixer, add the prepared flour mixture, then beat at low speed just until a thick, shiny batter forms. Do not overbeat—just moisten the flour. Remove the beaters and stir in the chocolate chips with a wooden spoon; or if the dough is too stiff, work them in by hand.

3. Scoop out a tablespoon of dough and roll it into a ball between your palms. Place it on a large, ungreased baking sheet, preferably nonstick; continue making these balls, spacing them about 1½ inches apart on the baking sheet. Gently press a cross-hatch pattern into each ball with a fork—do it gently, not until the sides crack.

4. Bake for about 11 minutes, or until lightly browned and set when touched, rotating the sheet once during baking. Cool the cookies on the baking sheet for 2 minutes, then transfer to a wire rack to cool completely. Cool the baking sheet for 5 minutes before making further batches, or use a second sheet that hasn't been in the oven.

Recommended storage
3 days at room temperature
2 months in the freezer

More Choices!

For cakier cookies, substitute 1 large egg and 1 large egg yolk for the 2 large egg whites, in the base recipe or any variation.

Double Peanut Butter Chocolate Chip Cookies: Reduce the semisweet chocolate chips to 1½ cups; add 1½ cups peanut butter chips with the remaining chips.

GORP Peanut Butter Chocolate Chip Cookies: Reduce the semisweet chocolate chips to 1 cup; add 1 cup peanut butter chips and 1 cup golden raisins with the remaining semisweet chocolate chips.

Peanut Butter and Banana Chocolate Chip Cookies: Reduce the semisweet chocolate chips to 1½ cups; add 1½ cups crushed banana chips with the remaining semisweet chips. Reduce the vanilla extract to 2 teaspoons; add 1 teaspoon banana flavoring with the remaining vanilla.

Peanut Butter White Chocolate Chip Cookies: Reduce the semisweet chocolate chips to 1½ cups; add 1½ cups white chocolate chips with the remaining chips.

Triple Peanut Butter Chocolate Chip Cookies: Reduce the semisweet chocolate chips to 1 cup; add 1 cup peanut butter chips and 1 cup roasted unsalted peanuts with the remaining chips.

PEPPERMINT CHOCOLATE CHIP COOKIES

Rather than simply flavoring the dough with peppermint extract, we make these with crushed peppermint candies for an added kick. But be careful: those tiny, hard pieces of candy aren't the best thing for bridgework or dentures.

MAKES ABOUT 3½ DOZEN COOKIES

- 1½ cups plus 2 tablespoons all-purpose flour
- ½ teaspoon baking soda
- ½ teaspoon salt
- ½ cup solid vegetable shortening (4 ounces)
- 8 tablespoons (1 stick) cool, unsalted butter, cut into small pieces
- ½ cup granulated sugar
- ¼ cup packed light brown sugar
- 1 large egg, at room temperature
- ½ teaspoon vanilla extract
- 2½ cups semisweet or bittersweet chocolate chips, or semisweet chocolate chunks
- 1⅓ cups crushed peppermint candies (see Note)

1. Position the rack in the middle of the oven. Preheat the oven to 350°F. Line a large baking sheet with parchment paper or a silicone baking mat; set aside. Whisk the flour, baking soda, and salt in a medium bowl until the soda is evenly distributed; set aside as well.

2. Soften the shortening and butter in a large bowl, using an electric mixer at medium speed, about 1 minute. Add both kinds of sugar; continue beating until light and fluffy, about 2 more minutes. Beat in the egg and vanilla until smooth. Turn off the mixer, add the prepared flour mixture, and beat at low speed just until moistened. Use a wooden spoon to stir in the chocolate chips and crushed peppermint candies just until evenly distributed.

3. Drop by tablespoonfuls onto the prepared baking sheet, spacing the mounds about 2 inches apart. Bake for about 12 minutes, rotating the sheet back to front halfway through baking. The cookies should be lightly browned and set. Cool on the baking sheet for 2 minutes, then transfer to a wire rack to cool completely. Cool the baking sheet for 5 minutes before baking further batches.

NOTE: *To crush the candies, place them in a zip-sealed plastic bag, then place them on the floor and whack them repeatedly with the bottom of a large, heavy saucepan. Continue crushing them until you have a good mixture of fine crumbs and slightly larger pieces, a little larger than coarse cornmeal.*

Recommended storage
4 days at room temperature between sheets of wax paper
2 months in the freezer

Mix It Up!

Spearmint Chocolate Chip Cookies: Substitute crushed spearmint hard candies or candy canes for the peppermint candies (do not use soft, Canadian mints or breath mints).

Wintergreen Chocolate Chip Cookies: Substitute crushed wintergreen candy canes for the peppermint candies.

POTATO CHIP CHOCOLATE CHIP COOKIES

This is one of those only-in-America recipes, claimed to have been invented by residents of many states—California, Georgia, Texas, to name a few. Like other homespun treats, the exact origins are hard to pin down. Suffice it to say, crushed potato chips make a very crunchy cookie. We've used margarine here, not butter, so that the taste of the potato chips really comes through.

MAKES ABOUT 4½ DOZEN COOKIES

1¾	cups all-purpose flour
½	teaspoon baking soda
½	teaspoon grated nutmeg
½	pound (2 sticks) cool margarine, cut into small pieces
1	cup granulated sugar
¾	cup packed dark brown sugar
1	large egg, at room temperature
1	large egg white, at room temperature
2	teaspoons vanilla extract
4	ounces potato chips, crushed (about 6 cups)
3	cups semisweet or bittersweet chocolate chips

1. Position the racks in the top and bottom thirds of the oven; preheat the oven to 350°F. Whisk the flour, baking soda, and nutmeg in a medium bowl until well combined; set aside.

2. Place the margarine in a large bowl and beat with an electric mixer at medium speed until softened. Add both kinds of sugar and continue beating until the mixture is homogenous but grainy, not smooth, with no bits of margarine visible, about 2 more minutes. Scrape down the sides of the bowl, beat in the egg, then the egg white and vanilla.

3. Turn off the beaters, add the flour mixture, and beat at low speed until a sticky and thick but nonetheless soft batter forms, about 20 seconds. Remove the beaters and stir in the crushed potato chips and chocolate chips with a wooden spoon, just until evenly distributed.

4. Drop by rounded tablespoonfuls onto two large ungreased baking sheets, preferably nonstick, spacing the mounds about 2 inches apart. Bake for 8 minutes, then reverse the baking sheets front to back and top to bottom. Continue baking for about 7 more minutes, or until the cookies are browned and somewhat firm to the touch. Cool on the baking sheets for 2 minutes, then transfer to wire racks to cool completely. Cool the baking sheets for 5 minutes before baking additional batches.

Recommended storage
4 days at room temperature
3 months in the freezer

Personalize It!

It's easy to vary this recipe—just use different types of potato chips. Don't be afraid to try making these cookies with sour cream and onion, salt and vinegar, or barbecue potato chips. We have and gotten rave reviews from friends.

You can also use the taro, sweet potato, beet, or turnip chips that are often seen in gourmet markets. Finally, for a crunchier texture, use thick-cut, wavy potato chips, such as Ruffles.

PUMPKIN CHOCOLATE CHIP COOKIES

So you don't want the standard pie for Thanksgiving? Watch the faces of your friends and family light up when you bring out a big platter of these moist cookies. Better yet, don't wait for the holidays!

MAKES ABOUT 4 DOZEN COOKIES

- 2 cups plus 2 tablespoons all-purpose flour, plus additional for dusting the baking sheets
- 1 teaspoon baking soda
- ½ teaspoon ground cinnamon
- ½ teaspoon grated nutmeg
- ½ teaspoon salt
- 8 tablespoons (1 stick) cool, unsalted butter, cut into small pieces, plus additional for greasing the baking sheets
- 1 cup packed light brown sugar
- ½ cup granulated sugar
- 1 large egg, at room temperature
- 1 large egg white, at room temperature
- ½ cup solid-packed canned pumpkin (do not use canned pumpkin pie filling)
- 2 teaspoons vanilla extract
- 3 cups semisweet or bittersweet chocolate chips

1. Position the racks in the top and bottom thirds of the oven; preheat the oven to 350°F. Lightly butter and flour two large baking sheets; set aside. Whisk the flour, baking soda, cinnamon, nutmeg, and salt until uniform; set aside as well.

2. Soften the butter in a large bowl, using an electric mixer at medium speed, about 1 minute. Add both kinds of sugar and beat at medium speed until light and airy, but still somewhat grainy, about 1 more minute. Beat in the egg and egg white until smooth, then beat in the canned pumpkin and vanilla. Don't worry if the dough looks slightly curdled at this point. Remove the beaters.

3. Stir in the prepared flour mixture with a wooden spoon or a rubber spatula, folding in even arcs until the flour is incorporated, but not until the batter turns sticky. The mixture should be soft and light, like a traditional chocolate chip cookie dough.

4. Drop by rounded tablespoonfuls onto the prepared baking sheets, spacing the mounds about 2 inches apart. Bake for 10 minutes, then reverse the baking sheets top to bottom and back to front. Continue baking for about 8 to 12 more minutes—the shorter time will produce soft, delicate cookies; the longer, crisp and crunchy ones. The cookies should be lightly browned and somewhat springy to the touch when done. Cool on the baking sheets for 2 minutes, then transfer to wire racks to cool completely. Cool the baking sheets for at least 5 minutes before buttering and flouring them again and baking additional batches.

Recommended storage
3 days at room temperature
3 months in the freezer

Customize It!

Substitute milk chocolate or white chocolate chips for the semisweet chocolate chips. Or reduce the chips, or any variety of chips, to 2 cups and add 1 cup of one of the following: chopped hazelnuts, chopped pecans, chopped roasted unsalted cashews, chopped roasted unsalted peanuts, chopped unsalted pistachios, chopped walnuts, or raisins.

For a truly over-the-top cookie, you can frost any of these variations with Marshmallow Fluff!

RATNER'S CHINESE COOKIES

Ratner's was once a Manhattan institution renowned for its soups and baked goods. It's long gone now, but here's a version of the famous cookies. They're probably called "Chinese" because of the almond flavoring. Here we coat them in sesame seeds for a truly exotic chocolate taste.

MAKES A LITTLE LESS THAN 5 DOZEN COOKIES

3	cups all-purpose flour, plus additional for dusting
½	teaspoon baking soda
⅛	teaspoon salt
¼	cup plus 2 tablespoons cocoa powder, preferably natural, sifted
3	tablespoons hot water
1	cup plus 3 tablespoons sugar
2	cups sesame seeds, preferably white sesame seeds
½	pound (2 sticks) cool, unsalted butter, cut into small pieces, plus additional for buttering the baking sheets
1	large egg, at room temperature
2	large egg whites, at room temperature
½	teaspoon almond extract
½	teaspoon vanilla extract

1. First, prepare the ingredients you'll need later on. Whisk the flour, baking soda, and salt in a medium bowl until the baking soda is evenly distributed; set aside. Mix the cocoa powder, hot water, and 3 tablespoons sugar in a small bowl until it forms a thick paste; set aside as well. Finally, sprinkle the sesame seeds on a large plate or cutting board and set aside.

2. Soften the butter in a large bowl, using an electric mixer at medium speed, about 1 minute. Add the remaining 1 cup sugar and beat until pale yellow and light, about 1 more minute. Beat in the egg, then one of the egg whites, the almond extract, and vanilla. Remove the beaters, scraping off any dough adhering to them.

3. Stir in the prepared flour mixture with a wooden spoon or a rubber spatula, just until a soft, moist dough forms.

4. Lightly dust a clean, dry work surface with flour, then divide the dough in half and place one half on the work surface. Dust the dough and a rolling pin with flour, then roll the dough into a 6 × 8-inch rectangle. Spread half the chocolate paste over this rectangle, leaving a ½-inch border around all sides. Roll up into a log, starting at one of the long sides—roll tightly without squeezing down.

5. Whisk the remaining egg white and 2 teaspoons cool water in a small bowl. Brush half this mixture over the log, then roll the log it in the sesame seeds, coating it with seeds (but leaving enough for the second log). Seal this log in plastic wrap and refrigerate until cold and firm, about 2 hours or up to 48 hours. Meanwhile, repeat the process to create a second chocolate-filled, sesame-coated cookie roll; seal this one in plastic wrap and refrigerate it, too.

6. Position the racks in the bottom and top thirds of the oven. Preheat the oven to 350°F. Lightly butter two large baking sheets.

7. Unwrap one of the cookie rolls and slice it into ¼-inch disks. Place the disks on the prepared baking sheets, spacing them about 1 inch apart. Bake for 7 minutes, then rotate the sheets back to front and top to bottom. Bake for another 6 to 8 minutes or so, until the cookies give a little when touched but are nonetheless firm. Cool on the baking sheets for 2 minutes, then transfer to wire racks to cool completely. If baking additional batches, cool the baking sheets for 5 minutes and lightly butter them again. You can also keep the dough logs in the refrigerator for up to 4 days, slicing off and baking as many cookies at a time as you like. Or you can freeze one of the logs for up to 1 month; if so, let it thaw in the refrigerator for 3 hours before slicing off the cookies and baking them.

> **Recommended storage**
> *4 days at room temperature*
> *Once baked, 3 months in the freezer*

SOFT CHOCOLATE CHIP OATMEAL COOKIES

Ah, soft, moist, classic oatmeal cookies—but with chocolate chips, not raisins! We've adjusted the sweetness to account for the chips; but in the end, these are the old standards, made better with chocolate.

MAKES ABOUT 4 DOZEN COOKIES

1	cup all-purpose flour
1	teaspoon ground cinnamon
½	teaspoon baking soda
½	teaspoon salt
12	tablespoons (1½ sticks) cool, unsalted butter, cut into small pieces
1	cup packed dark brown sugar
3	tablespoons granulated sugar
1	tablespoon light corn syrup
1	large egg, at room temperature
1	large egg white, at room temperature
2	tablespoons milk (regular, low-fat, or nonfat)
2	teaspoons vanilla extract
3	cups rolled oats (do not use quick-cooking oats)
3	cups semisweet or bittersweet chocolate chips

1. Position the rack in the center of the oven. Preheat the oven to 350°F. Whisk the flour, cinnamon, baking soda, and salt in a medium bowl until the cinnamon and soda are evenly distributed; set aside.

2. Soften the butter in a large bowl, using an electric mixer at medium speed, about 1 minute. Add both kinds of sugar and the corn syrup; continue beating at medium speed until soft, light, and pale brown, about 2 more minutes. Beat in the egg, then the egg white, milk, and vanilla until smooth. Turn off the beaters, add the prepared flour mixture (in stages, if necessary), and beat at low speed just until incorporated. Stir in the oats and chocolate chips with a wooden spoon until the chips are evenly distributed.

3. Drop by rounded tablespoonfuls onto a large ungreased baking sheet, preferably nonstick, spacing the mounds about 2 inches apart. Bake for 6 minutes, rotate the baking sheet front to back, and continue baking for about 7 minutes, or until the cookies are lightly browned, somewhat soft, but definitely set. Cool on the baking sheet for 1 minute, then transfer the cookies to a wire rack to cool completely. Cool the baking sheet for 5 minutes before baking another batch, or use a second baking sheet that hasn't been in the oven.

Recommended storage
5 days at room temperature
Not recommended for freezing

Customize It!

Reduce the semisweet or bittersweet chocolate chips to 1½ cups and add 1½ cups of any of the following, or a combination of any of the following: butterscotch chips, chopped pecans, chopped walnuts, dried cranberries, M&Ms, milk chocolate chips, peanut butter chips, raisins, Reese's Pieces, roasted unsalted peanuts, sweetened shredded coconut, or white chocolate chips.

SPUMETTI

These crisp meringue cookies are popular in Italy at Christmastime. They're best dipped in sweet wine, red wine, or a strong cup of coffee. You'll need four large baking sheets to make this recipe: you bake two sheets, then let the cookies cool completely on those sheets, meanwhile baking two more sheets. Why not just use two sheets? Since the cookies take a while to cool, it would be unsafe to leave the egg-white mixture at room temperature for all that time. Do not refrigerate the egg-white-and-cocoa mixture or it will lose its silky texture and the cookies will turn gummy.

MAKES ABOUT 4½ DOZEN COOKIES

3	cups whole hazelnuts (about ¾ pound), toasted and skins removed (see page 96 for instructions on toasting the hazelnuts)
4	large egg whites, at room temperature
½	teaspoon salt
½	teaspoon cream of tartar
4¼	cups confectioners' sugar (1 pound)
2	tablespoon cocoa powder, preferably natural, sifted
1	teaspoon ground cinnamon

1. Place 2 cups of the hazelnuts in a food processor fitted with the chopping blade; pulse a few times to grind the nuts into coarse pieces; set aside. Cut the remaining nuts in half; set aside as well.

2. In a dry, large, clean bowl, beat the egg whites and salt with an electric mixer at high speed until foamy. Add the cream of tartar and beat until the cream of tartar is dissolved into the mixture, just until it's opaque, about 15 seconds. Do not make a meringue with peaks; do not let the egg whites begin to billow up with air. Mix in the confectioners' sugar, cocoa powder, and cinnamon; beat at medium speed until the mixture looks like thick, sticky canned frosting, about 6 minutes.

3. Beat in the coarsely chopped hazelnuts; continue beating for 3 minutes until the mixture is sticky, wet, and gooey. Mix in the remaining halved hazelnuts. Cover the mixture with a clean kitchen towel and let stand at room temperature for 20 minutes to begin to firm.

4. Meanwhile, position the racks in the top and bottom thirds of the oven; preheat the oven to 325°F. Line two large baking sheets with parchment paper or silicone baking mats; set aside.

5. Scoop up a small amount of the chocolate mixture, about 2 teaspoons' worth, and drop it on one of the prepared baking sheets, making a little mound. Continue making these, spacing them about 1½ inches apart until the sheets are filled. Bake for 20 minutes, then reverse the sheets back to front and top to bottom. Continue baking for about 10 to 15 more minutes until the cookies are browned, dried out, and firm. Cool completely on the baking sheets before removing and storing. Bake additional batches on separate, lined baking sheets, as needed.

Recommended storage
1 week at room temperature
Not recommended for freezing

SWEET POTATO CHOCOLATE CHIP COOKIES

Sweet potatoes add a wonderful delicacy to chocolate chip cookies. We've even added some Marshmallow Fluff for that familiar Thanksgiving-sweet-potato-casserole taste.

MAKES ABOUT 4 DOZEN COOKIES

One 8-ounce sweet potato
2	cups all-purpose flour
½	teaspoon baking soda
½	teaspoon ground cinnamon
½	teaspoon salt
¼	teaspoon grated nutmeg
12	tablespoons (1½ sticks) cool, unsalted butter, cut into small pieces
½	cup granulated sugar
½	cup packed light brown sugar
⅓	cup Marshmallow Fluff
1	large egg, at room temperature
2	teaspoons vanilla extract
2½	cups semisweet or bittersweet chocolate chips

1. Position the racks in the top and bottom thirds of the oven; preheat the oven to 400°F.

2. Place the sweet potato in a shallow roasting pan or casserole dish and bake for about 1 hour and 15 minutes in the top third of the oven, until soft and wrinkly. Cool on a rack for 15 minutes, or until you can handle the potato, then cut it in half and scoop the flesh into a medium bowl. Mash with a fork; set aside to cool as you prepare the dough. You should have about ⅔ cup mashed sweet potato.

3. Reduce the oven temperature to 350°F. Whisk the flour, baking soda, cinnamon, salt, and nutmeg in a medium bowl until uniform; set aside.

4. Beat the butter in a large bowl, using an electric mixer, until softened. Add the granulated sugar and brown sugar; continue beating until the mixture is homogenous, with no bits of butter visible, but still a little grainy if rubbed between your fingers, about 2 minutes. Beat in the Marshmallow Fluff, then scrape down the sides of the bowl and beat in the egg until smooth. Beat in the mashed sweet potato and vanilla, about 10 seconds.

5. Turn off the beaters, add the flour mixture, and beat at low speed until a soft, smooth batter forms, about 15 seconds. Stir in the chocolate chips with a wooden spoon, just until evenly distributed.

6. Drop by rounded tablespoonfuls onto two large ungreased baking sheets, preferably nonstick, spacing the mounds about 1½ inches apart. Bake for 8 minutes, then reverse the sheets back to front and top to bottom. Continue baking for about 7 more minutes, or until the cookies are springy to the touch but nonetheless set and browned. Cool on the baking sheets for 2 minutes, then transfer to a wire rack to cool completely. Cool the baking sheets for 5 minutes before baking additional batches.

> **Recommended storage**
> *3 days at room temperature*
> *2 months in the freezer*

More Choices!

Sweet Potato Almond Cranberry Chocolate Chip Cookies: Reduce the chocolate chips to 1 cup; add ¾ cup slivered almonds and ¾ cup dried cranberries with the remaining chips.

Sweet Potato Banana Macadamia Nut Chocolate Chip Cookies: Reduce the chocolate chips to 1 cup; add ¾ cup crushed banana chips and ¾ cup chopped unsalted macadamia nuts with the remaining chips.

Sweet Potato Ginger Cashew Chocolate Chip Cookies: Reduce the chocolate chips to 1 cup; add ¾ cup finely chopped crystallized ginger and ¾ cup chopped roasted unsalted cashews with the remaining chips.

Sweet Potato Walnut Raisin Chocolate Chip Cookies: Reduce the chocolate chips to 1 cup; add ¾ cup chopped walnuts and ¾ cup raisins with the remaining chips.

TOFU CHOCOLATE CHIP COOKIES

Here, tofu replaces eggs for these cakey but light cookies. But don't make them just for dietary reasons. These moist, delicious cookies are a comforting treat right out of the oven. Don't even tell your kids they're eating healthfully!

MAKES ABOUT 4 DOZEN COOKIES

Nonstick baking spray
1   cup whole wheat flour
1   cup all-purpose flour
½   teaspoon baking soda
½   teaspoon salt
8   tablespoons (1 stick) cool margarine, cut into small pieces
½   cup packed light brown sugar
½   cup granulated sugar
6   ounces silken firm tofu (about ¾ cup, see Note)
1   teaspoon vanilla extract
3   cups semisweet or bittersweet chocolate chips, or chocolate chunks

1. Position the racks in the top and bottom thirds of the oven. Preheat the oven to 375°F. Spray two large baking sheets with nonstick spray; set aside. Whisk the whole wheat flour, all-purpose flour, baking soda, and salt in a medium bowl until uniform; set aside as well.

2. Beat the margarine and both sugars in a large bowl, using an electric mixer at medium speed; continue beating until smooth and light, about 2 minutes.

3. Place the tofu in the bowl of a food processor fitted with the chopping blade. Pulse two or three times, then process until the tofu is about the consistency of mashed potatoes. It will look a little curdled, broken, and lumpy.

4. Add the mashed tofu to the butter and sugar mixture; beat at medium speed until smooth, about 1 minute. Scrape down the sides of the bowl, then beat in the vanilla. Turn off the beaters, add the prepared flour mixture (in stages, if necessary), then beat at a very low speed, just until a loose, wet, but nonetheless firm dough forms. Gently stir in the chocolate chips.

5. Drop by rounded tablespoonfuls onto the prepared baking sheets, spacing the mounds 2 inches apart. Bake for 7 minutes, then rotate the sheets back to front. Bake for about 7 more minutes, or until the cookies are lightly browned, set, but still soft. Cool on the baking sheets for 2 minutes, then transfer to wire racks to cool completely. Cool the baking sheets for 5 minutes before baking additional batches.

NOTE: *Tofu is packaged and sold based on its texture: firm, extra-firm, or silken. To complicate matters, some silken tofu is now sold as "firm silken," meaning that it has slightly more tooth than run-of-the-mill silken varieties. This latter type, such as that sold under the brand Mori-Nu, is best for this recipe, although any silken tofu will do.*

Recommended storage
3 days at room temperature
2 months in the freezer

Personalize It!
Reduce the chocolate chips to 1½ cups and add 1½ cups of any of the following or any combination into the batter with the remaining chips: chopped dried apples, chopped dried figs, chopped dried pears, chopped pitted dates, chopped pitted prunes, dried blueberries, dried cherries, dried cranberries, sesame seeds, unsalted sunflower seeds.

TRIPLE CHOCOLATE
CHOCOLATE CHIP COOKIES

These cookies are a chocolate lover's dream come true. Semisweet and unsweetened chocolate are in the dough, as well as cocoa powder. Surprisingly, the cookies are not as sweet as you might imagine, so every bite has an intense chocolate hit. Oh, and we've thrown in chocolate chips, just for good measure.

MAKES ABOUT 4 DOZEN COOKIES

1½	cups all-purpose flour, plus additional for dusting the baking sheet
⅓	cup cocoa powder, preferably natural, sifted
½	teaspoon baking soda
¼	teaspoon salt
8	ounces semisweet chocolate, chopped
3	ounces unsweetened chocolate, chopped
12	tablespoons (1½ sticks) cool, unsalted butter, cut into small pieces, plus additional for greasing the baking sheet
1	cup packed dark brown sugar
½	cup granulated sugar
2	large eggs, at room temperature
2	large egg whites, at room temperature
1	teaspoon vanilla extract
2	cups semisweet or bittersweet chocolate chips

1. Position the oven rack in the middle of the oven; preheat the oven to 325°F. Lightly butter and flour a large baking sheet; set aside. Whisk the flour, cocoa powder, baking soda, and salt in a medium bowl until uniformly colored; set aside as well.

2. Place the semisweet and unsweetened chocolate in the top half of a double boiler set over about 1 inch of simmering water, or in a medium bowl that fits very tightly over a medium saucepan with about the same amount of simmering water. Stir until half the chocolate has melted, then remove the double boiler's top half or the bowl from the heat and continue stirring until all the chocolate has melted. Transfer to a clean, dry bowl and set aside to cool for 5 minutes.

3. Meanwhile, soften the butter in a large bowl, using an electric mixer at medium speed, about 1 minute. Add the brown sugar and granulated sugar; continue beating until fluffy, if still a little grainy, about 1 more minute. Beat in the whole eggs one at a time, making sure the first is thoroughly incorporated before adding the second. Beat in the egg whites and vanilla until smooth. Turn off the beaters, add the prepared flour mixture, and beat at low speed just until a thick, dry dough forms. Stir in the chocolate chips with a wooden spoon.

4. Drop by rounded tablespoonfuls onto the prepared baking sheet. Bake for 10 minutes, then rap the pan against the oven rack or the oven door, giving it two or three good smacks. (Make sure you use hot pads or wear oven mitts!) Reverse the baking sheet front to back, then continue baking for about 6 more minutes, or until the cookies are bumpy yet springy, with some spreading at the edges. Cool on the baking sheet for 5 minutes, then transfer to a wire rack to cool completely. Cool the baking sheet for about 5 minutes before buttering and flouring it again and baking further batches.

Recommended storage
3 days at room temperature
3 months in the freezer

More Choices!

Quadruple Chocolate Chocolate Chip Cookies: Reduce the semisweet chocolate chips to 1 cup; add 1 cup white chocolate chips with the remaining semisweet chips.

Quadruple Chocolate Mint Chocolate Chip Cookies: Reduce the semisweet chocolate chips to 1 cup; add 1 cup mint chocolate chips with the remaining semisweet chips.

Triple Chocolate Coconut Chocolate Chip Cookies: Reduce the semisweet chocolate chips to 1 cup; add 1 cup sweetened shredded coconut with the remaining semisweet chips.

Triple Chocolate Peanut Butter Chocolate Chip Cookies: Reduce the semisweet chocolate chips to 1 cup; add 1 cup peanut butter chips with the remaining semisweet chips.

VEGAN CHOCOLATE CHIP COOKIES

Our problem with most of the vegan chocolate chips cookies you buy in grocery stores and gourmet markets? They're too soft and cakey, not at all like the classic cookies. So here's our answer: tahini, oats, and maple syrup, all of which produces a crunchy vegan cookie that's so good you'll never miss the dairy and eggs.

MAKES ABOUT 4 DOZEN COOKIES

- 2 cups all-purpose flour
- 1 cup rolled oats (do not use quick-cooking oats)
- 1 teaspoon baking soda
- 1 teaspoon salt
- 12 tablespoons (1½ sticks) cool margarine, cut into small pieces, plus additional for the baking sheet
- ½ cup tahini (see Note)
- 1 cup sugar
- ½ cup maple syrup
- 1½ tablespoons vanilla extract
- 3 cups bittersweet or semisweet chocolate chips

1. Position the rack in the center of the oven; preheat the oven to 350°F. Whisk the flour, oats, baking soda, and salt in a medium bowl until uniform; set aside. Grease a large baking sheet with a dab of margarine on a crumpled piece of wax paper or the wrapper from the margarine itself; set aside as well.

2. Beat the margarine and tahini in a large bowl with an electric mixer at medium speed until smooth and fairly creamy, about 2 minutes. Add the sugar and beat until thick and smooth, about 1 minute. Add the maple syrup and vanilla; beat just until incorporated. Remove the beaters.

3. Stir in the flour mixture, using a wooden spoon or a rubber spatula, just until incorporated and no traces of flour remain. Do not beat. Stir in the chocolate chips.

4. Scoop out a rounded tablespoon of the dough and roll it into a ball between your palms. Place on the prepared baking sheet and continue rolling balls of dough, spacing them 1½ inches apart on the baking sheet. Press the balls with your thumb, just to flatten slightly. Bake until light brown and firm to the touch, about 12 minutes. Cool the cookies for 2 minutes on the baking sheet, then transfer them to a wire rack to cool completely. Cool the baking sheet a few minutes before continuing with the next batch of cookies.

NOTE: *Tahini is a sesame-seed paste sold in most supermarkets. The oil can separate from the paste; if this occurs, you have to work to stir it back into suspension, cutting the paste first with a fork, then stirring with a spoon. We prefer resealable jars for better storage—which should always be done in the refrigerator. Always smell tahini before using, to make sure the paste hasn't developed a bitter aroma during long storage.*

Recommended storage
4 days at room temperature
3 months in the freezer

Mix It Up!

For cakier cookies, freeze the rolled balls before you bake them, at least 8 hours, until hard. Place the frozen balls on the baking sheets, spacing them about 2 inches apart. Add 1 or 2 minutes to the baking time.

For a little chewier cookie, substitute honey for the maple syrup.

For an even chewier cookie, substitute honey for the maple syrup, and peanut butter (do not use "natural" peanut butter) for the tahini.

VIENNESE CHOCOLATE PEPPER COOKIES

These thin cookies, spiked with black pepper, have long been a favorite in Viennese cafes. They're spicy and delicious—perhaps a little exotic. Best of all, you can make the dough log in advance and store it for up to 4 days in your refrigerator, slicing off cookies and baking them at will.

MAKES ABOUT 3 DOZEN COOKIES

1½	cups all-purpose flour, plus additional for dusting the work surface
¾	cup cocoa powder, preferably Dutch-processed, sifted
1	teaspoon baking powder
¼	teaspoon salt
12	tablespoons (1½ sticks) cool, unsalted butter, cut into small pieces, plus additional for greasing the baking sheets
1	cup granulated sugar
1¼	teaspoons freshly ground black pepper
¼	teaspoon ground allspice
1	large egg, at room temperature
2	teaspoons vanilla extract
2	tablespoons confectioners' sugar

1. Whisk the flour, cocoa powder, baking powder, and salt in a medium bowl until uniform; set aside.

2. Soften the butter in a large bowl, using an electric mixer at medium speed, about 1 minute. Add the granulated sugar and beat until light and fluffy, if still a little gritty, about 2 minutes. Beat in ¾ teaspoon of the pepper and the allspice. Scrape down the sides of the bowl, then beat in the egg and vanilla until smooth, about 1 minute. Turn off the mixer, stir in the prepared flour mixture, and beat at low speed just until there are no white streaks in the batter.

3. Dust your work surface lightly with flour, then turn the dough onto it. Roll gently into a 9-inch log, wrap it in plastic wrap, and refrigerate until firm, about 3 hours.

4. Position the racks in the top and bottom thirds of the oven. Preheat the oven to 375°F. Lightly butter two large baking sheets; set aside.

5. Slice the log into ¼-inch-thick cookies; place these about 1 inch apart on the prepared baking sheets. Bake for 6 minutes, then rotate the baking sheets top to bottom, turning each front to back. Continue baking for about 6 more minutes until the cookies are slightly puffed and the tops feel springy when touched. Cool for 2 minutes on the baking sheets, then transfer the cookies to wire racks to cool completely. Cool the baking sheets for at least 5 minutes before baking a second batch; then grease them again before proceeding.

6. Once all the cookies are fully cooled, mix the confectioners' sugar with the remaining ½ teaspoon black pepper. Place this mixture in a fine-mesh strainer and sift it lightly over the cookies, giving them a fine coating.

Recommended storage
5 days at room temperature
3 months in the freezer

WHITE CHOCOLATE ALMOND RASPBERRY COOKIES

These crisp cookies are extraordinarily sweet, with the great taste of raspberry jam folded into the batter. Use a good-quality raspberry jam; if yours has seeds, press it through a fine-mesh strainer to get rid of them—you'll need about ⅔ cup seeded jam to make ½ cup seedless.

MAKES ABOUT 4½ DOZEN COOKIES

2	cups all-purpose flour
1	teaspoon baking soda
½	teaspoon baking powder
¼	teaspoon salt
6	ounces white chocolate, chopped
1	cup whole almonds
1	cup sugar
8	tablespoons (1 stick) cool, unsalted butter, cut into small pieces, plus additional for greasing the baking sheets
½	cup seedless raspberry jam
1	large egg, at room temperature
2	teaspoons vanilla extract

1. Position the racks in the top and bottom thirds of the oven; preheat the oven to 350°F. Lightly butter two large baking sheets; set them aside. Whisk the flour, baking soda, baking powder, and salt in a medium bowl until uniform; set aside as well.

2. Place the white chocolate, almonds, and ½ cup of the sugar in a food processor fitted with the chopping blade; pulse several times to break up the almonds, then process just until the mixture is finely ground. You may need to stop the machine once or twice, scrape down the sides, and rearrange the larger pieces to chop them thoroughly. Don't process too long or the chocolate will begin to melt and turn the mixture gooey.

3. Soften the butter in a large bowl, using an electric mixer at medium speed, about 1 minute. Add the remaining ½ cup sugar and continue beating until soft and fluffy, about 1 minute. Beat in the raspberry jam, then the egg and vanilla. Beat in the ground white chocolate mixture just until incorporated. Turn off the beaters, add the prepared flour mixture (in stages, if necessary), and beat at low speed just until a stiff, thick, pastelike dough forms. If you're using a handheld mixer, the dough may be too stiff—so stir in the flour mixture with a wooden spoon just until the flour is incorporated.

4. Pinch off walnut-size pieces of the dough and place them about 1½ inches apart on the prepared baking sheets. Press each piece of dough with a fork into a cross-hatch pattern, pressing down just so the sides begin to crack and the cookie flattens somewhat.

5. Bake for 8 minutes, then reverse the sheets top to bottom and back to front. Continue baking for about 7 more minutes, or until the cookies are lightly browned but still somewhat soft to the touch. Cool for 2 minutes on the baking sheets, then transfer to wire racks to cool completely. Cool the baking sheets for 5 minutes before buttering again and baking further batches.

Recommended storage
4 days at room temperature
3 months in the freezer

Customize It!
Substitute any of the following for the raspberry jam: apricot jam, blueberry jam, cloudberry jam, ginger jam, grape jam, seedless blackberry jam, or strawberry jam.

WHITE CHOCOLATE
CHOCOLATE CHIP COOKIES

Here's a surprise: a white chocolate cookie that's crisp, not gummy. For best results, use a fine-quality white chocolate, not cut with stabilizers and hydrogenated vegetable shortening.

MAKES ABOUT 5 DOZEN COOKIES

2	cups all-purpose flour
1	teaspoon salt
½	teaspoon baking soda
8	ounces white chocolate, chopped
12	tablespoons (1½ sticks) cool, unsalted butter, cut into small pieces
½	cup granulated sugar
⅓	cup packed light brown sugar
1	large egg, at room temperature
1	large egg white, at room temperature
2	teaspoons vanilla extract
3	cups semisweet or bittersweet chocolate chips

1. Position the rack in the top third of the oven; preheat the oven to 325°F. Whisk the flour, salt, and baking soda in a medium bowl until well combined; set aside.

2. Place the white chocolate in the top half of a double boiler set over a pot with about 2 inches of simmering water, or in a large bowl that fits tightly over a large pot with about the same amount of simmering water. Stir until half the white chocolate has melted, then remove the double boiler's top half or the bowl from the heat and continue stirring until all the white chocolate has melted. Set aside to cool for 5 minutes.

3. Place the butter in a large bowl and beat with an electric mixer at medium speed until softened, about 1 minute. Add both kinds of sugar and continue beating until the mixture is light but not smooth, with no bits of butter visible but the sugar still partially undissolved, about 1 minute. Beat in the egg, then the egg white until smooth. Scrape down the sides of the bowl, then beat in the cooled, melted white chocolate, pouring it into the mixture in a thin, steady stream while the beaters are running at medium speed. Beat until smooth, about 20 seconds, then beat in the vanilla.

4. Turn off the beaters, add the flour mixture, and beat at low speed or stir with a wooden spoon until a soft, pliable, but somewhat sticky batter forms, about 15 seconds. Stir in the chocolate chips with a wooden spoon just until evenly distributed.

5. Drop by rounded tablespoonfuls onto a large, ungreased baking sheet, preferably nonstick, spacing the mounds about 2 inches apart. Bake in the top third of the oven for 8 minutes, then reverse the sheet front to back. Continue baking for about 8 more minutes, or until the cookies are soft but set, very lightly browned at the edges. Cool on the sheet for 2 minutes, then transfer to a wire rack to cool completely. Cool the sheet for 5 minutes before baking additional batches.

> **Recommended storage**
> *4 days at room temperature*
> *3 months in the freezer*

More Choices!

Black and White Chocolate Chocolate Chip Cookies: Reduce the semisweet chocolate chips to 1½ cups; add 1½ cups white chocolate chips with the remaining semisweet chips.

Cherry White Chocolate Chocolate Chip Cookies: Reduce the semisweet chocolate chips to 1½ cups; add 1½ cups dried cherries with the remaining semisweet chips.

Pure White Chocolate Chocolate Chip Cookies: Substitute white chocolate chips for the semisweet chips.

White Chocolate Walnut Milk Chocolate Chip Cookies: Substitute 1½ cups chopped walnuts and 1½ cups milk chocolate chips for the semisweet chips.

WHOOPIE PIES

Whether you call them Moon Pies, Scooter Pies, or Whoopie Pies, they're an American classic: big cookie sandwiches with marshmallow cream centers. What a fitting end to a chocolate cookie book! Even better, freeze them and eat them right out of the freezer—think of them as frozen candy bars.

MAKES 8 LARGE SANDWICH COOKIES

FOR THE COOKIES

2	cups all-purpose flour
1	cup cocoa powder, sifted
½	teaspoon baking soda
¼	teaspoon salt
½	cup solid vegetable shortening (4 ounces), plus additional for greasing the baking sheets
1	cup packed dark brown sugar
¼	cup granulated sugar
1	large egg, at room temperature
2	teaspoons vanilla extract
½	cup buttermilk (regular or low-fat, but not nonfat)

FOR THE FILLING

¼	cup solid vegetable shortening (2 ounces)
3	tablespoons unsalted butter, at room temperature
1	cup confectioners' sugar
1	tablespoon vanilla extract
⅛	teaspoon salt
⅓	cup Marshmallow Fluff

1. Position the racks in the top and bottom thirds of the oven; preheat the oven to 350°F. Whisk the flour, cocoa powder, baking soda, and salt in a medium bowl until uniformly colored; set aside. Use a dab of shortening on a piece of crumpled wax paper to grease two large baking sheets; set aside as well.

2. Beat the shortening, brown sugar, and granulated sugar in a large bowl, using an electric mixer at medium speed, until light and fluffy, about 2 minutes. Scrape down the sides of the bowl, then beat in the egg and vanilla. Beat in ¼ cup of the buttermilk until smooth, then remove the beaters. Stir in half the prepared flour mixture with a wooden spoon, then stir in the remaining ¼ cup buttermilk. Finally, gently stir in the remainder of the flour just until incorporated. The dough will be thick and wet. Do not overmix.

3. Scoop up ¼ cup of the dough and place it on one of the prepared baking sheets. Use your fingers or a wet rubber spatula to flatten it gently into a disk about 3 inches in diameter and ½ inch high. Continue making these disks, spacing them about 3 inches apart on the two baking sheets. You should have enough dough for about 16 unbaked cookies—make an even number so you can turn them all into sandwich cookies.

4. Bake for 8 minutes, then rotate the sheets top to bottom and back to front. Continue baking for about 7 minutes, or until the cookies are dry on the surface but still soft to the touch. Cool for 3 minutes on the baking sheets, then use a metal spatula to transfer them to a wire rack to cool completely.

5. Once the cookies are cooled, make the filling: beat the shortening and butter in a medium bowl with an electric mixer at medium speed until uniform. Beat in the confectioners' sugar until light and fluffy, about 1 minute. Beat in the vanilla and salt. Finally, scrape down the sides of the bowl and beat in the Marshmallow Fluff.

6. Place 2 tablespoons of this filling in the center of the flat side of one cookie. Drag the icing toward the cookie's edges, using an icing knife or a rubber spatula, taking care that the cookie is completely coated with the filling. Top the iced cookie with a second cookie, flat side down. Continue until all the Whoopie Pies are made, placing them on a wire rack for about 30 minutes, until the filling firms a bit.

Recommended storage
2 days at room temperature
2 months in the freezer

SOURCE GUIDE

American Spoon Foods
P.O. Box 566
Petoskey, MI 49770
1-800-222-5886
www.spoon.com
Tons of dried fruits, nuts, and preserves

Broadway Panhandler
477 Broome Street
New York, NY 10013
1-866-COOKWARE or 1-212-966-3434
www.broadwaypanhandler.com
Muffin tins, mixers, spatulas, wooden spoons, mixing bowls, sifters, and just about anything else you need for making muffins

Kalustyan's
123 Lexington Avenue
New York, NY 10016
1-212-685-3451
www.kalustyans.com
The place for international one-stop shopping, including nut oils, exotic flours, flavorings, and dried fruits

King Arthur Flour
Norwich, VT
1-800-827-6836
www.kingarthurflour.com
Not only great flour, but a catalog with hard-to-find items like rye flour, cherry or cinnamon chips, and maple sugar

Kitchen Market
218 Eighth Avenue
New York, NY 10011
1-888-408-4433
A great source for Latin American and Mexican foods, including chiles and spices

Marshall's Honey Farm at the Flying Bee Ranch
155-159 Lombard Road
American Canyon, CA 94503
1-800-624-4637
www.MarshallsHoney.com
The best honey of all varieties from apiaries in northern California

New York Cake and Baking Distributors
56 West 22nd Street
New York, NY 10010
1-212-675-CAKE or 1-800-942-2539
Every baking tool imaginable, including a
wide range of baking sheets

Penzeys
P.O. Box 924
Brookfield, WI 53088
1-800-741-7787
www.penzeys.com
Incredibly fresh spices and some of the best
vanilla extract available

Scharffen Berger Chocolate Maker, Inc.
914 Heinz Avenue
Berkeley, CA 94710
1-800-930-4528
www.scharffenberger.com
One of America's premier chocolate
makers—and premier cocoa nibs makers

Williams-Sonoma
P.O. Box 7456
San Francisco, CA 94120
1-800-541-2233
www.williams-sonoma.com
Mixers, bowls, baking pans, and many
flavorings from a national retail chain

www.ultimatecook.com
Recipes and information on the *Ultimate*
books, on Bruce and Mark, on our hard-
cover title *Cooking for Two*, and a list of
links to some of our favorite mail-order
sources

INDEX

cranberry:
  chocolate chews, 52
  chocolate oatmeal almond cookies,
    129
  sweet potato almond chocolate chip
    cookies, 214
cream cheese:
  chocolate chip refrigerator cookies,
    76
  in chocolate coconut cookies, 68–70
  in chocolate Hanukkah gelt, 76
  chocolate mint refrigerator cookies,
    76
  chocolate refrigerator cookies,
    75–76
  chocolate refrigerator sandwich
    cookies, 76
  in chocolate rugelach, 148–49
  filling, for chocolate pinwheels,
    138–40
crinkles, chocolate, 80
"crunch-o-meter," 5–6
currant(s):
  chocolate chip biscotti, 54
  chocolate madeleines, 109
  chocolate pinwheels, 140
  in mole cookies, 195–96

daiquiri-coconut chocolate chip
    cookies, 170
dairy-free cookies, 23
  chocolate almond horns, 44–45

chocolate chews, 51–52
chocolate chip, 171–72
chocolate chip meringues, 55–56
chocolate coconut macaroons,
    71–72
chocolate cream sandwich, 77–79
chocolate fortune, 82–83
chocolate gingerbread men, 84–86
chocolate gingersnaps, 87–88
chocolate hazelnut biscotti, 93–95
chocolate meringues, 120–21
chocolate mint sandwich, 124–25
chocolate sandies, 150–51
chocolate snickerdoodles, 154–55
chocolate tea, 160–61
French macaroons, 175–76
fudge meringues, 179–80
low-fat chocolate biscotti, 189–90
nearly nonfat chocolate, 197–98
potato chip chocolate chip, 203–4
spumetti, 211–12
tofu chocolate chip, 215–16
vegan chocolate chip, 219–20
dates:
  chocolate oatmeal pecan cookies,
    129
  chocolate spiced refrigerator
    cookies, 147
dipped cookies:
  almond coconut, 26–28
  chocolate biscotti, 47–48
  chocolate coconut macaroons, 72

chocolate marshmallow, 112–14
espresso chocolate chip biscotti, 174
Mexican chocolate, 194
double banana chocolate chip cookies, 30
double boiler, 15
double chocolate coconut cookies, 70
double peanut butter chocolate chip cookies, 200
dropped cookies, 23–24
  big soft chocolate, 31–32
  black black and whites, 33–35
  brownie drops, 36–38
  butterscotch chocolate chip, 39–41
  chocolate chews, 51–52
  chocolate chip meringues, 55–56
  chocolate chip oatmeal, 57–58
  chocolate chocolate chip, 59–60
  chocolate chunk, 61–62
  chocolate coconut and pecan, 66–67
  chocolate coconut macaroons, 71–72
  chocolate meringues, 120–21
  chocolate molasses raisin, 126–27
  chocolate oatmeal raisin, 128–29
  classic chocolate chip, 167–68
  coconut chocolate chip, 169–70
  fudge meringues, 179–80
  ginger chocolate chip, 183–84
  honey chocolate chip, 187–88
  maple chocolate chip, 191–92
  nearly nonfat chocolate, 197–98
  peppermint chocolate chip, 201–2

  potato chip chocolate chip, 203–4
  pumpkin chocolate chip, 205–6
  soft chocolate chip oatmeal, 209–10
  spumetti, 211–12
  sweet potato chocolate chip, 213–14
  tofu chocolate chip, 215–16
  triple chocolate chip, 217–18
  white chocolate chip, 225–26

eggs, temperature of, 11
electric mixers, 12–13, 16
equipment, 14–16
espresso:
  chocolate chip biscotti, 173–74
  fudge meringues, 180

fillings:
  for chocolate coconut cookies, 68–70
  for chocolate cream sandwich cookies, 77–79
  for chocolate hazelnut sandwich cookies, 96–98
  for chocolate Linzer cookies, 104–6
  for chocolate peanut butter cream sandwiches, 133–35
  for chocolate pinwheels, 138–40
  ganache, for chocolate ravioli cookies, 143–45
  ganache, for chocolate truffle sandwich cookies, 162–64
  for whoopie pies, 227–28

and seeds chocolate chip cookies, 188

walnut chocolate chip cookies, 188

horns, chocolate almond, 44–45

ice cream sandwiches, 32

jam:
    cream sandwiches, chocolate peanut
        butter and, 135
    thumbprints, chocolate, 99–101

kitchen scales, 12, 16

lace sandwich cookies, chocolate,
    102–3
lemon ginger chocolate chip cookies,
    184
lime chocolate coconut cookies, 70
Linzer cookies:
    chocolate, 104–7
    chocolate mint, 107
    chocolate orange, 107
    chocolate raspberry, 107
    chocolate rum, 107
low-fat chocolate biscotti, 189–90

M&M chocolate meringues, 121
macadamia (nuts):
    banana white chocolate chip
        cookies, 30
    in chocolate lace sandwich cookies,
        103

sweet potato banana chocolate chip
    cookies, 214
macaroons:
    chocolate coconut, 71–72
    French, 175–76
madeleines:
    chocolate, 108–9
    chocolate chip, 109
    chocolate currant, 109
    chocolate orange, 109
Mallomars, for fried chocolate
    cookies, 177–78
mandelbrot, chocolate, 110–11
maple extract:
    in butterscotch maple chocolate chip
        cookies, 41
    in chocolate maple refrigerator
        cookies, 147
maple sugar, in maple chocolate chip
    cookies, 191–92
marble refrigerator cookies:
    chocolate almond, 123
    chocolate banana, 123
    chocolate mint, 122–23
    chocolate orange, 123
    chocolate raspberry, 123
    chocolate rum, 123
marshmallow cookies, chocolate,
    112–14
Marshmallow Fluff:
    in chocolate fluffernutter cream
        sandwiches, 135

Nutella, in chocolate hazelnut
    sandwich cookies, 96–98

pepitas, in mole cookies, 195–96

pepper cookies, Viennese chocolate, 221–22

peppermint chocolate chip cookies, 201–2

piña colada:
  chocolate chip cookies, 170
  chocolate cookies, 70

pineapple coconut chocolate chip cookies, 170

pinwheel cookies:
  chocolate, 138–40
  chocolate apple, 140
  chocolate coconut, 140
  chocolate currant, 140
  chocolate pecan, 140

pistachio:
  chocolate oatmeal apricot cookies, 129
  coconut cookies, 28

pocket cookies, stuffed:
  chocolate almond, 50
  chocolate caramel, 49–50
  chocolate cherry, 50
  chocolate chestnut, 50
  chocolate hazelnut, 50
  chocolate Kiss, 50

potato chip chocolate chip cookies, 203–4

potato starch, in gluten-free chocolate chip cookies, 185–86

pretzels, chocolate, 141–42

pumpkin chocolate chip cookies, 205–6

quadruple chocolate chocolate chip cookies, 218

quadruple chocolate mint chocolate chip cookies, 218

raisin cookies:
  chocolate molasses, 126–27
  chocolate oatmeal, 128–29
  chocolate oatmeal cashew, 129
  chocolate oatmeal walnut, 129
  sweet potato walnut chocolate chip, 214

raspberry:
  chocolate Linzer cookies, 107
  chocolate marble refrigerator cookies, 123
  jam, in white chocolate almond raspberry cookies, 223–24
  liqueur, in cat's tongues, 42–43

Ratner's Chinese cookies, 207–8

ravioli cookies, chocolate, 143–45

Reboul, Pierre, 177

refrigerator cookies:
  chocolate, 146–47
  chocolate almond, 147
  chocolate almond marble, 123
  chocolate banana marble, 123
  chocolate cashew, 147
  chocolate chip cream cheese, 76

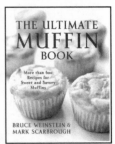
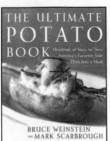

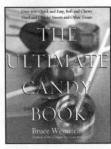
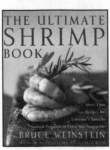
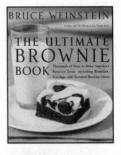
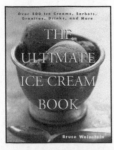